THE
MOUNTAIN BIKE
MANUAL

Dennis Coello

1985
Dream Garden Press
Salt Lake City

for Daryl

Copyright © 1985 by Dennis Coello and Dream Garden Press.
Equipment illustrations copyright by the manufacturer.

Manufactured in the United States of America.

Library of Congress Number: 85-071153

ISBN: 0-942688-26-0

Book Design and Mountain Bike logo by Richard Firmage

First Edition   A B C D E F G H

Dream Garden Press • P.O. Box 27076 • Salt Lake City, UT 84127

FOREWORD

Mountain Bikes: they come equipped as trail bikes—ready for wet sand, desert scrub, the unpaved road. Change the tires and you're set for all-terrain touring—fast travel on highways, plus freedom to roam the countryside. Or slap on a pair of fenders and hit the city streets; potholes won't break your spokes, flats are a thing of the past, and curbs can be hopped easily when the need arises.

All-terrain. All-season, All-purpose. And *all* of it fun.

But you can't use these beauties to their potential until you understand them—what makes them different from regular touring bikes, how to adapt them for various terrains, what accessories are available and which are necessary for each kind of riding. Part One of this book examines the bike in detail, in language that's easy to understand. You'll learn how to buy the best machine for your money, and how to upgrade a lesser bike in the least expensive way. From basic frames to panniers and rearview mirrors, you'll know your bike—and every item made for it.

Part Two is pure mechanics. How to go about making your gears work again—when you've been trail riding and can't see your chain for the mud. How to replace a spoke that's eaten a rock, how to pull maintenance on wheel bearings and bottom brackets, and how to remove your handlebars for airline travel. Detailed drawings will make disassembly easy, even if you've never handled a wrench. And the book has been kept small and light, so it'll be with you on the road when you need it.

In short, this is a manual as all-purpose as the bikes.

Dennis Coello
St. Louis

ACKNOWLEDGMENTS

I wish to express my gratitude for the efforts of the following individuals and companies in providing illustrations and art work: Nate Bischoff, Dennis Nieweg, Mary Perkins, Gary Marcus / SHIMANO, Ellen Gruber / SPECIALIZED, Thomas Franges / SUNTOUR, Peter Hlavacek / TREK.

Also, a special note of thanks to Peter Hlavacek, for his assistance in several expeditions; to Art Edison, Bopsy Coello, Doug Conners, Daryl Schueller, Bob Welsh, and Gary Topping for sharing the trails; to Marc Brown, Ken Sanders, and Dick Firmage of Dream Garden Press; and last of all to the thirty-odd manufacturers of bikes, bags, components and accessories who have supplied test equipment, listened to my criticisms, and produced for us all a brand new cycling experience.

Note to Consumers:

In the following pages you will encounter many brand names. I say good things about some, bad things about others. But there's a problem: products can change quickly, while books remain the same.

My solution to this difficulty has been to discuss—often in generic terms—the merits and defects of those items necessary to the mountain biker. Such information will help you become a discriminating buyer. So read carefully, balance merits and defects and cost, and *never* buy by name alone. (Well, except perhaps in authors. . . .)

In this way you'll choose wisely, spend little, and never feel compelled to wring my neck for leading you astray.

CONTENTS

THE
MOUNTAIN BIKE
MANUAL

PART ONE

CHAPTER ONE

"BUT I'VE ALREADY GOT A BIKE!"

Ten years ago I pedalled the Southwest on a touring bike. It was the final leg of a world ride. I'd ridden along the Seine, the Nile, and the Mekong; galloped a camel around the Sphinx, and watched the sun rise and set over the vast, steamy fields of India. Beautiful. Fascinating. Romantic. But there was a problem. There were always so many *people*.

Things were different stateside. There were open, uninhabited spaces, privacy, and room to breathe. But upon my return I found that I couldn't ride to many of these areas—not on my touring bike. The multitudes of Asia and senses-numbing traffic of our West Coast made me wish I could leave the pavement behind. I began to find nothing so alluring as our own near-trackless deserts, and the occasional winding, rolling road of dirt or sand or slickrock. Quiet, solitude, and an uncluttered view of the natural setting often seemed just out of reach.

During later tours of the Midwest and East I found the same to be true; unpaved, nearly traffic-free roads led to the areas I wished most to visit. Some were historical and led to pioneer and cavalry trails, abandoned forts, ghost towns, mining camps and Indian battlegrounds. Some were scenes of natural wonder. But I couldn't pedal my touring bike to these sites, for the thin tires would sink in the dirt or sand, and the rigid, lightweight frame would first jar loose my fillings, then collapse under the strain.

Nor was backpacking the answer, for it was impossible to carry sufficient quantities of food and water for the long distances involved. (Since my Army days I've also hated the mule-like feeling of sixty pounds on my back.) Even passenger cars couldn't travel many of these unpaved roads, for fear of broken tie rods and perforated gas tanks. All were excluded, apparently, except jeeps and horses.

But then came the mountain bike.

I was skeptical when I first heard of "all-terrain" or "mountain bikes." After all, I hadn't owned a car for a decade, and had depended solely on my touring bike for transportation. Besides, the things looked so ungainly. Monster bikes, I thought. Gadgets for grown-ups, expensive toys designed with company profits—not road performance—in mind.

My difficulties with these newcomers were basic. For years the industry had been stressing lighter frames and components, and aerodynamic designs. Agility and efficient travel were the result. But these new ATBs brought vivid recollections of my childhood coaster-bomber, which went anywhere but rode like a dead horse and weighed about the same. Granted, I was intrigued by the promise of off-road travel, of riding on the beach, and of being impervious to the sewer gratings and chuckhole-hazards of city streets. But *not* at the cost of riding a fifty pound paperboy bike. Fortunately, I decided to take a closer look.

"Evolution at its best!" my friend announced, as we walked around his bike shop. As both salesman and mechanic he knew ATBs inside and out.

"You've got the same reservations I had at first," he assured me. "But here, look at this."

As we examined the bikes he explained how the industry had applied all its new technology to strike the perfect balance for on- *and* off-road travel. I listened, became interested when I lifted the bike and found it very light, and responded quickly to his offer of a test ride.

"It'll feel odd at first, I guarantee it," he told me. "So give it a while. Don't come back for an hour. And above all don't baby it!"

I wheeled the bike outside, feeling a bit like a man coming home from the pound with a Doberman. I knew I was *supposed* to be in command, but.... Swinging a leg over its back I grabbed the huge, soft, motorcycle-style handgrips, placed a foot on the massive bear-trap pedal, and on the first downstroke lifted myself into the saddle.

It *was* odd. I felt like George Washington in all those old paintings, sitting ramrod-straight on his horse; no foreign-style paperclip curl for the rider on these things. That'll please a lot of folks, I thought, who complain of backaches and neckaches and a persistent inability to get used to dangling over the handlebars of touring bikes. I felt like I was sitting at the breakfast table.

Suddenly, while looking down at the chainring, I was served a curb. From the sidewalk in front of the shop I'd been rolling slowly toward the street. My many years of skinny-wheeled riding had of course taught me *never* to drop off a curb. Unless you like replacing spokes on the freewheel side, or feeling a blip in your rim forevermore.

Quickly pulling to a stop, I glanced at the rear wheel. What I saw reassured me. Huge, thick-treaded knobbies. Spokes that looked like gleaming pencils, and a rim the width of my forearm. Well, I thought, this could be fun.

The next hour of my life was one of those wonderful, memorable bundles of time, a sweet combination of exciting events and pleasant emotions. I hopped curbs. I aimed at chuckholes. I stormed the steepest hills I could find. And—I'm ashamed to say—I even pulled a lawn job. I felt as free, as sure-footed, as lightning-quick as a squirrel. And the queer thing was that I actually felt *safer* on this two-wheeled jeep than on my touring bike.

Why? I studied the question as I pedalled back to the shop. The answers were obvious. First, my hands had never left the handlebars. Thumb-operated bar-mount shifters allowed effortless gear changing. The oversize brake handles were also always in reach, and the huge cantilever brakes were more than a match for the large rims. Strong, wide pedals with bear-trap edges made for a firm grip. And the lack of a toeclip and strap combined freedom of movement with sure footing.

The upright handlebars—which make these bikes look so "head-heavy" (like a Texas longhorn) also contribute to safety. Because the rider isn't perched over the bars he can slam on the brakes or hit a hole at full speed without fear of flipping over the front wheel. The wide, nearly straight bars also provide the rider with an amazing degree of control. (Picture a three-foot long bit in a horse's mouth, and the leverage you'd exert when tugging on the reins.)

During that hour-long ride I tested the bike on turns, increasing my speed as my confidence grew. Finding that my position in the saddle—closer to the ground and farther back from the bars—allowed me to lean into turns far more than normal, I searched for the kind of street corner which the careful touring cyclist dreads. You know the ones—filled with gravel and a half-inch of dirt, sprinkled lightly with tab tops and glass, and usually avoided at all costs. If the rider is forced by traffic to ride through it he'll be lucky not to gain a nasty slit in his tire. (Before puncture-resistant tubes and tire liners he would have had a flat as well.) Yet the real problem comes when road debris is collected at the corner where the biker makes his turn; especially if slick, the tire can slide laterally through the gravel and dirt and bring on a fall.

I wanted to see how mountain bikes would handle such situations. Pretending that it was night, that I was in a hurry, that I didn't know the road and was therefore riding fast and blind, I raced into the turn.

The first time I coasted through it quickly. The second time I continued pedalling as the rear tire hit the debris. And the third time I pretended someone had stepped off the curb in front of me, that cars were at my side in the turn and that my only choice was the brakes. A *sure* "go-down" scenario in a tight lean, an instance when one must decide between mowing down the pedestrian or eating one's handlebars on the way to the ground.

Amazing. I had complete control during the first two runs, and good control on the third. I sprayed some gravel out behind me when I threw on the brakes, and felt the rear wheel bounce lightly, then return to ground and find its grip again. The knobby treads held fast, and upon inspection showed little damage from the glass. (I've since had many occasions to run such corners in rain; the big tires handle even these conditions well. They're also too wide to fall into those horrible sewer gratings.)

Finally, my sense of safety was increased by the ability, whenever I wished, to leap up on the sidewalk. Knowing I wouldn't damage the bike, and learning quickly how to pull back on the bars as I pumped down on the pedals, I found that I could leave a too-busy street at will.

"So how'd you like it?" my friend asked, as I wheeled the bike inside. His face wore the crafty smile of the salesman sure of a sale.

"Not bad," I answered, assuming the usual equivocal tone of a customer about to bargain. "Not bad at all."

The hook had been set. That much was obvious. But I was still troubled by the thought that this was—for me—a luxury. I already had an excellent touring bike. Although the new breed was plainly much safer for city travel, I was a very careful and veteran cyclist. (I hadn't always been that way; getting plastered twice by huge Buicks had *made* me careful.)

Still, the undeniable *fun* of riding these new bikes . . . and the ability, at long last, to pedal all those traffic-free dirt roads was attractive. But could I tour on it? Would it be too slow for long-distance commuting? What about the increased wind resistance of upright bars? Were there trails I could ride without doing ecological damage? And how did one know what constituted a *good* mountain bike?

A hundred questions troubled me back then. But they've all been answered during a year of daily commuting, many week-long back-country trips, and five long months of all-terrain touring.

So whether you're still just thinking about a mountain bike, or want to get the most out of the one you own, read on. And welcome to a brand new world of biking.

CHAPTER TWO

CHOOSING YOUR MOUNTAIN BIKE

People spend weeks deciding which lawnmower, typewriter, washing machine or car will grace their lives for a few years. They read about them, look at them in various stores, and compare models, prices, and warranties. But when it comes to a bike, something that will likely outlast almost everything else a person buys, things are different.

Maybe it's because there's no motor to listen to, no door to slam to see if the thing is solid. And of course kicking the tires is out. But I suspect it has more to do with people seeing bikes as kids' stuff. That is, until they walk into the bike shop. And then they're bewildered with head tube angles, chainstay lengths and five-pin spiders. Dazzled with such wizardry they go with what the salesman says, or buy the brand mentioned by a friend.

It's a pity. Chances are you won't be fleeced if you do this, for most shops are fair and honest. But it's pure luck if you stumble onto the bike that's best for you.

So what's the answer? An extremely detailed analysis of options at this point would probably leave you as perplexed as would the salesman's verbal presentation. But you *should* know what to look for, what to avoid, and which features are important to the kind of riding you'll be doing. And you need to understand the terminology involved.

What follows, therefore, is a simple but comprehensive explanation of mountain bike theory and design. Take your time and read carefully. This is, after all, one purchase which will last a lifetime.

Frame
Dress up an old paperboy bike frame with the best components and wheels around, and you'll still have a bike that rides like a World War

One tank. Those old indestructibles gained their strength from sheer mass; the heavy frame tubes of low-grade carbon steel began life as flat sheets of metal, which were then rolled and welded. This long weld-line generated the term "seamed" tubing—industry shorthand for "strength-through-weight."

"Seamless" tubing is produced by the precision piercing of a solid cylinder of steel. This technique is generally employed with a better quality metal and is usually referred to by frame builders as "high-tensile" steel. These tubes are lighter—due to thinner walls, and stronger—due to the absence of a seam and the better quality carbon steel used. Department store bikes often use seamed tubes, while most lower to mid-range bikes sold in bike shops will be seamless carbon steel.

The next great leap forward in frames—and generally upward in price as well—is to to the more exotic alloys. "Chro-mo" and "chrome-moly" refer to the most common of this upper tier of frames, and are abbreviated terms for "chrome-molybdenum alloy steel." Sometimes the manufacturer's name is employed to designate the materials, as in top-of-the-line Reynolds 531 (manganese-molybdenum), Ishiwata, Columbus, and others. But don't let the names trip you up. For example, Ishiwata makes both a chrome-moly and a carbon-manganese frame. Carbon-manganese is of lesser quality. Not much less, and therefore unimportant unless you've decided upon bike racing as a career. But is shouldn't cost you quite as much as chrome-moly or manganese-molybdenum.

Now don't start crying. Just think of it like this: seamed tubing is out; high-tensile seamless is okay but not as good as the steel alloys of carbon-manganese (better), and either chrome- or manganese-molybdenum (best). See? No need for tears. Besides, we're not finished yet.

Frame tubes receive their greatest stress near their ends. Manufacturers can therefore save considerable weight and still retain strength by making the tube walls thin in the middle, thicker at the ends. This process is known as "butting." Those frames which are not butted (or "double-butted" as it is often called) are termed "straight-gauge," a reference to the single wall thickness throughout the tube. Butted tubing is both preferable to straight-gauge and more expensive.

One way to increase the strength of a mountain bike without using expensive butted tubes is to employ tubing which is larger in diameter. Compare an ATB with a touring bike and you'll notice the "beefy" look which the larger frame tubes impart. Such oversize tubes are necessary with mountain bikes, to handle the severe strain imparted by hard trail riding. Those who plan to really thrash their bikes should go the final step to butted, oversize tubes.

And a final word on composition. Be prepared to hear a salesman say something like "chrome-moly main tubes, high-tensile fork and stays." This means just what it says; the main triangle—top, down and seat tubes—is chrome-moly, but the fork, seatstays and chainstays are not. Your considerations in such a case should be the extra weight (not great), slightly less strength, and a smaller price tag than a bike which is described as "chrome-moly throughout."

Frame Geometry

The next topic in the discussion of frames is geometry. Sure it's a horrible thought. Brings back memories of high school theorems and polygons, doesn't it? Well, all we need here is a bit of vocabulary and some generally accepted truths on angles and wheelbase. Get this much and—just like in school—you can forget the rest.

Study the drawing. You frame sophisticates will notice I've left off such things as "trail" and "front center"—because they're unnecessary in choosing the right bike. But some, like seat and top tube lengths, *are* critical in buying a bike that fits.

FRAME GEOMETRY

A Seat tube length
B Seat tube angle
C Head tube angle
D Top tube length
E Chainstay length
F Fork rake
G Bottom bracket height
H Wheel base

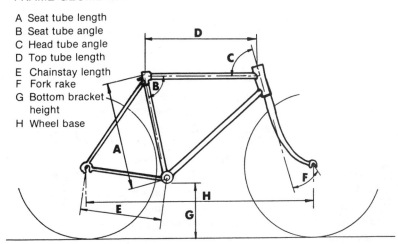

Most shops will fit a person to a touring bike by having them straddle the bike, stand flat-footed over the top tube in shoes with a moderate heel (no pumps or sandals, unless you plan always to ride in them), and check to see that there's a clearance of 1″ to 1½″. Too short a bike and you'll feel cramped; too tall and you'll hurt yourself on the top tube.

But the proper fit on an ATB—where it's likely you'll be coming out of the saddle more often—is somewhat different. I say *somewhat* because it really depends upon how you use your mountain bike. I ride mine mostly on pavement—in city travel and while touring—and less on dirt roads and trails. Therefore I want a larger frame than if I rode primarily in dirt. (Smaller, shorter frames are more easily negotiated in rough country.) Riding a 25½″ touring frame, I chose a 24″ mountain bike. This provides me with two full inches of clearance while still permitting full leg extension when pedalling easy roads. If most of my riding was done off-road I'd have gone to a 23″ or 22″ frame, raising the extra-long seat post (common to mountain bikes) when on pavement.

Arm and leg lengths are generally proportionate. Therefore, a tall person requiring a long seat tube (which determines the frame size) will also need a long top tube. If the top tube is too long the rider will have difficulty in reaching the handlebars; too short and the rider will find himself hanging over the bars. On touring bikes a longer or shorter handlebar stem can be used to correct for top tube length. Mountain bikes do not offer this alternative, and it is therefore critical to buy correctly. My suggestion is to begin by determining frame size and then to ride several different brands to get the feel of various top tube lengths. (One would expect to find a close correlation between seat and top tube lengths with all manufacturers; this is not yet true.)

Mountain bikes generally have a longer wheelbase and less steep head and seat angles (see drawing) than do touring bikes. The theory is that a longer wheelbase aids in slow-pedalling comfort and handling, but detracts from agility in high-speed handling. Having said this, I suggest you leave theory behind and base your purchase once again on the careful test riding of several brands and models. Why? Because otherwise you'll go nuts, especially when you find that a 67° head angle on one brand frame performs like a 70° head angle on another. Besides, detectable riding differences are most often rather insignificant.

If, however, you are oriented toward more analytical problem solving, try this. Once again determine what style of riding you'll do most often. Obtain the technical specification charts on the models of ATBs in your price range and test ride those bikes which have the most appropriate frame geometry. For example: I will spend most of my time on pavement and relatively hard-packed dirt roads. I therefore want a bike with a long wheelbase, and less steep angles. Wheelbases generally run from 40″ to 46″ (with exceptions); head angles from 67°

to 71½° (again with exceptions). (We won't worry about seat angles, as they parallel the head angle on a frame, i.e., a steep head angle frame generally has a steep seat angle as well.) However, I'll be in rough country perhaps one-third of the time, and therefore need a bike which doesn't make such travel too difficult.

The solution? Using wheelbase as the primary determinant, I test ride all bikes in the 43" to 46" range. Not worrying about head and seat angles, I go with the bike which feels best, so long as the chainstays are long enough for panniers (about 17½" minimum—if they are this short you might want to mount your bags to see if your heels clear when pedalling), and the bottom bracket height is sufficient to clear most rocks and curbs (around 11" minimum). If it's been a rough and thorough test ride, I know I've got the best all-round frame.

There are a few additional frame-related features you should notice:

a) *fork blades*—like the seat and chainstays, these should be larger than on a touring bike.

b) *reinforced seat tube*—to facilitate the repeated use of the quick-release seat post, without damaging the seat post neck.

c) *braze-ons*—top tube cable guides (preferably on *top* of the tube for easier carrying); down tube cable stops; water bottle and rack mounts; chain hanger (holds the chain in place when rear wheel is off the bike). Unlike "a" and "b" above, braze-ons are a valuable *luxury*, which should be expected to increase a frame's overall cost.

Wheels

There should be few non-negotiable demands on your part when you begin looking for a mountain bike. You might trade off chrome-moly for lower cost, or trade color choice for best wheelbase. But if you plan to spend anywhere from $275 and up for your bike, be sure it has alloy—not steel—rims. The reason is "rolling weight"—the all-important fact that weight on the wheels is far more critical than weight anywhere else on the bike. Why? Because an extra ounce on the wheel must be pushed around in a circle *and* down the road; an ounce on the frame travels only its linear path. In addition, alloy rims are stronger and stop better when wet.

Far less critical is the fact that more expensive bikes sport chrome-moly axles and hubs, in place of lower-priced (and lesser strength) carbon steel. Most mountain bikes come with "sealed" hubs, necessary to protect against the onslaught of mud and water which off-road use entails. (A special but inexpensive and easily obtainable tool is necessary to service some of these hubs.) I haven't found a difference in performance between large- or small-flange hubs on mountain *or* touring bikes; likewise I would not be concerned with spoke size (most common is 14 gauge) or lacing pattern. Good mountain bike rear wheels are made with reduced "dishing" (the sharper degree at which the freewheel-side spokes must attach to the hub to compensate for the width of the freewheel). This helps greatly in reducing spoke breakage.

I'll have more to say about tires in the next chapter; for now I'll merely suggest that you again keep rolling weight in mind, and opt for skinwall (rather than heavier gumwall) construction.

Bars/Stem

Some "half-breed" bikes are offered with flat, steel handlebars and stems. A single test ride will show you how much stress is concentrated in this area, and thus most true ATBs sport a "triangulated" bar/stem arrangement. Once more the chrome-moly bars and alloy stems are preferable (in both strength and weight) to steel.

Crankset

If at all possible, spend the extra money for a forged alloy, one-piece right arm/spider crankset. ("Spider" refers to the attachment piece radiating from the right crankarm to the chainrings. Choose a five-pin spider—five metal attachment arms—over a three, for durability.) Lesser bikes are equipped with stamped steel cranks. The difference is easy to detect while riding, for, after hard use, out-of-true chainrings will bring on the noise of derailleur cage/chain contact, and a certain overall feeling of sloppiness in pedalling.

Crankarms also come in various lengths. The most standard—170mm—is thought best for bikes which will be used primarily on pavement. Long arms of 180mm are thought to assist in climbing steep, off-road hills. The theory is that the shorter arm allows a faster spin (pedalling or cyclic rate) to be maintained, while the longer arm provides greater leverage. Yet a problem lurks: a longer crankarm allows less ground clearance—an important factor in off-road riding. Some companies are playing it safe by equipping their bikes with 175mm arms, thus splitting the difference.

But for the average rider we're splitting hairs. Ten millimeters is less than half an inch, hardly a critical difference for riders who'll be using a single bike on all terrains. My personal feeling is that we need to know such things so as to knowledgeably gauge their importance—or unimportance—to our kind of riding. Cycling abounds with bike-shop bikers who think *every* technical advantage is a must. These folks are valuable for their earnestness and understanding of mechanics. Don't buy until you understand what they're saying; compare notes from different shops. But then decide for yourself what *you* need on *your* bike.

A far more important topic than crankarm length is gearing. Most ATBs have triple cranks (three chainrings), so as to gain the very low end of a wide range of gears. But all triples are not created equal, and you need to understand gearing to know why.

In an earlier book on touring bikes I explained this subject in the following manner:

Many bike manufacturers publish literature on their cycles which state something like "33 to 101 gear range as equiped," or "100 inch gear high range." What is a 100 inch gear, and how is that number derived? It comes from this formula:

$$\frac{\text{\# teeth in front sprocket}}{\text{\# teeth in rear sprocket}} \times \text{wheel diameter in inches}$$

Take my touring bike for example: the large front sprocket has 54 teeth, the smallest back sprocket has 14.

$$\frac{54}{14} \times 27 = 104 \text{ inch gear}$$

But this does *not* mean the bike will travel 104 inches down the road with one pump of the pedals. It refers instead to the number of inches in diameter the front wheel would be in a "direct-drive" set-up, such as the old "high-wheelers" during the 1870s and 1880s. Those bikes had no complicated gearing, and therefore the single "gear" was determined by the size of the front wheel, to which the pedals were attached. Imagine a high-wheeler 104 inches in diameter, or more than 8½ feet high!

On the other end of the scale the lowest gear on my bike is 33.3 inches:

$$\frac{42}{34} \times 27 = 33.3$$

In this case the "high-wheeler" wouldn't be so high at all, and would look more like a child's tricycle. Now you can see the beauty of today's gearing, which provides for such extremes of great speed and hill climbing potential, and all the ratios between.

Because dirt roads and trails are often far steeper than anything paved, mountain bikes are geared much lower than the normal touring bike. I can recall thinking my 24″ low gear rather silly at first, when I was getting to know the bike around the neighborhood. And then I rode sixty miles of dirt and sand and slickrock in southern Utah, through the desert to the Colorado Gorge. Sand-choked washes and steep canyon walls taught me to appreciate that gear, and to suggest that if the triple crankset you're about to purchase can't get you down

into the middle 20s (see gear chart in appendix), don't buy it.
Most freewheels on ATBs have five or six sprockets, with the largest
cog a 32 or 34 tooth. If the specification chart doesn't show it, ask the
salesman to work out the gear range with you; some less expensive
triples will accept nothing smaller than a 32 or 34 tooth inner chainring.
The resultant 1 to 1 gear ratio—great in a touring bike—just isn't low
enough for off-road/dirt road riding. (I'll discuss extending the high
range of gear ratios in Chapter Four.)

I've already talked about the importance of sealed bearings in wheel
hubs. The bottom bracket—the axle or "spindle" to which the crankarms are attached—can also take a terrific beating from the elements.
So appreciate a sealed bottom bracket if it comes your way, and expect
to pay more for it. Personally, if I had to make a choice between sealed
wheel hubs or bottom bracket, I'd choose the wheels. Cotterless crank-
sets (minus cotter pins, employing bolts to attach the crankarms—the
only style to buy and almost invariably the system offered these days)
are a snap to service. (See Part Two.)

Brakes

Cantilevers are a must. Avoid those huge sidepulls like the plague,
for the result will be the same. Only cantilevers have the necessary
strength, for the width of the tire and rim requires a sidepull to be so
large that it becomes unwieldly. (The long metal arm and single
attachment point places too great a strain on a sidepull.)

Begin your search for good brakes by looking at a pair on a top-of-
the-line bike. They'll be made of a forged aluminum alloy (rather than
pressed steel), and the "mounting shaft axles" will be brazed or welded
for added strength onto the frame mount bosses. If the terminology is
difficult even after glancing at the "Cantilever Brake Assembly" section
diagram in the appendix E, merely ask the salesman if his bikes' brakes
are welded. If he says yes, ask him to point out the frame boss. If he
doesn't know what you're talking about find someone who does.

High-priced brakes also come with large, easily gripped motorcycle-
style levers, heavy duty cables, and long, adjustable brake pads. Pay
great attention to such things, for they can be of critical importance.
Lesser-grade components elsewhere on the bike will reduce performance, or require additional care. Poor brakes, however, can get you
killed.

Derailleurs

Once again alloy is preferable to steel, for better performance,
greater strength, and less weight. Various manufacturers offer a "moun-

tain series" line of derailleurs, in which the shifting mechanisms are sealed against dirt. These are by far the best, and are well worth the relatively slight additional cost. (At present you'll find the excellent Shimano or SunTour derailleurs on most mountain bikes; their performance, even when obscured by mud, is phenomenal.)

Rough road and off-road riding requires one's hands to be always on the bars. That means down tube, stem and bar-end shifters are out. Designers have answered the problem with one of the most functional features of a mountain bike—thumb shifters. While even the low-end ATBs have thumb-operated controls, you should, while test riding, run through the gears several times to make sure everything is working properly.

Seatpost/Saddle

A relatively unnoticed item on touring bikes, the seatpost on an ATB—when ridden in rough, unpaved terrain—becomes crucial. It must be very strong to withstand the rider's weight bouncing upon it. (The strength can come from lightweight alloy, or thick-walled, heavy steel.) And it must be long enough to allow for full leg extension (a critical consideration due to the shorter than normal frames on mountain bikes).

Some bikes also have a quick-release skewer directly beneath the saddle (in addition to the *almost* standard *and* requisite quick-release seatpost lever in the frame), to adjust the saddle's forward-backward position. I find this an unnecessary feature for my style of riding, though I do like the option of making this adjustment easily on those posts fitted for an allen wrench (like the Sakae "Laprade").

I hesitate to say much of anything about saddles, due to the extremely personal nature of this component. Most mountain bikes come equipped with padded, "anatomically designed" saddles, with slightly different shapes for men and women. Less expensive seats have a heavy steel under-carriage; better saddles are made of alloy. (See Part Two for further discussion of this topic.)

Pedals

This is another category in which you should begin your search with the best. Why? Because, like brakes, a few models come equipped with pedals which actually make riding dangerous. Some pedals, like the SunTour XC-II, are wide, shaped like bear traps, and sealed. The spindle (pedal axle) is chrome-moly, the frame a light but strong alloy, and a toe clip and reflector can be added. But the pedal is not safe merely because of its strength; the combination of its width and trap-like teeth—which grip the soles of *any* shoes—provides very secure footing. Of course, you can always upgrade to these or a similar model. Saving a gram here and there does add up; the overall weight on the best non-custom bikes is right around thirty pounds (22" frame). Most will fall into the thirty-two to thirty-four pound range, and are still a world apart from the old fat tire one-speed klunkers which tipped the scales at fifty.

Finally, remember to take your time in choosing your bike. Run through this chapter again, making a list of those items which appear most important to your anticipated riding needs. As you visit various shops to gather specification charts and to test ride the bikes, jot down on paper the individual costs of features. This may sound terribly time-consuming, but if done systematically it will prove a fast and simple method of making your choice. And you'll have a ready-made shopping list of those items you may wish in the future to upgrade.

CHAPTER THREE

PREPARING FOR THE TRAIL

I mentioned in Chapter Two that most mountain bikes are equipped for the trail when sold. Those with bear-trap pedals and large knobby tires will of course be much easier to handle in rough country, as discussed earlier. And hard-packed dirt roads are more quickly traversed with the slimmer, higher pressure road/trail tires which I examine in Chapter Four. But by and large your mountain bike, no matter the brand, is ready for the trail when you wheel it out of the shop.

This doesn't mean, however, that *you* are. For example, there are the questions of your riding skills, your ability to repair your bike if something breaks while you're off-road, and what to carry for the scrapes and cuts which come more often in the wild. Finally, *where* can you ride legally, and without doing environmental damage?

Let's deal with the last problem first. In February of '84, while cycling across the Southwest, I took a long side trip to view the cliff dwellings in the Gila National Forest. In conversation with rangers there I learned that a large group of mountain bikers had appeared several weeks before, determined to ride the trails through the adjoining wilderness area. They were informed that such travel is illegal in:

a) *wilderness areas:* means of "mechanical transport" in such areas is disallowed by the Gila Wilderness Act of 1964,

b) *national parks:* except on roads, and those paths specifically marked "bike path,"

c) *national forests:* except on roads and in those areas specified for "multiple use,"

d) *national monuments:* except on roads open to the public,

e) *most state parks and monuments:* except on roads and paths specifically marked "bike path."

(Now don't get upset; there are plenty of places left to ride and we'll get to them shortly.)

The rangers told me some of the bikers became indignant. "We don't do as much damage as horses!" one cried, and several spoke of their "right" to ride the trails. Another biker said he had heard of a recent change in the ruling, but the ranger was ready with a reply. Apparently this rumor of a change was widespread, and brought about the following clarification:

> A bicycle is a form of mechanical transport the use of which is prohibited in wilderness by Section 4(c) of the Wilderness Act and Title 36 CFR 293.6. The fact that the "enforcement regulation" was moved from the status of a mandatory regulation in Subpart A of CFR 261 to a discretionary regulation in Subpart B did not make bicycling a legal use within wilderness. It simply gave Supervisors discretion on how they approach the problem—by education and discouragement of occasional use, or by use of a law enforcement punishment approach through CFR 261.

In short, the action was still illegal. Only the park supervisor's *reaction* had been made discretionary.

So the law is clear. But should it be changed? After all, the Wilderness Act was passed long before mountain bikes were on the scene. And what of the issue of the comparative damage done by horses? And the more sticky problem of one's "right" to use a trail?

The National Off Road Bicycle Association (NORBA) has tried to gain access to wilderness trails. They approached the Sierra Club in hope of support for their lobbying efforts, but were rebuffed. The reasons given by the Sierra Club are interesting, and center around trail damage: soil erosion and deep tire ruts on steep portions of the paths, and new tracks made between turns when mountain bikers couldn't follow the switchbacks. Park rangers have told me of their fear for the "fragile ecosystems" easily damaged by bikers who ride the trails for the thrills involved in fast turns, sharp climbs and breakneck speed descents. They argue that horses generally remain on the paths and travel at a leisurely pace, neither of which is true for many mountain bikes. "Most people agree that motorized dirt bikes should be kept off the trails," a ranger told me at California's Anza-Borrego Desert State Park. "Well," she continued, "there's not much difference in the damage done by one of them and by ten mountain bikes."

But beyond ruts and soil erosion is the effect produced merely by the appearance of a bike in the wilderness. On many occasions—while hiking in the Wind Rivers, ski touring in Utah, and squirrel hunting in the deep woods of Missouri—I've quietly cursed the jet flying silently overhead. Though unheard and having no impact upon the trail, I perceive these mechanical devices as intruders. In this day of man's increasingly mechanical approach to the outdoors, when thousands experience nature not for what it is through observation but as a playground, there aren't many places left where one is guaranteed one won't be run over by a jeep or snowmobile or mountain bike. Preserving those areas—at the cost of a disgruntled few—seems worth the price.

I might add that cycle magazines do little to assist the off-road bikers' image with the public when they publish such articles as "Log Jumping for Trail Riders" (*Bicycling* June '84). This piece is illustrated with "six distinct steps in a log crossing," which picture the combatants in full color. The moss-covered log is a lovely medley of dappled browns and greens, a forest behemoth surrounded by its fellow trees and lime-colored ferns. In the other corner is the biker, dressed in helmet, gloves, blue skin suit and knee and shin pads—looking more prepared for a moon shot than a ride in the countryside.

Later in the article we're warned that if our ATB has large chainrings we should take them off, lest we "wreck them." Nothing is said about the damage done to the "recreational" log while we're wrecking our chainrings on it, or the result of dragging a lubricated chain across the moss. Granted, the forest area pictured is no doubt "legal" for mountain bikes. And it may even be just a small wooded piece of land on the edge of a subdivision. But other visitors—no matter the area—should be able to rest themselves without fear of getting grease on their pants.

And if the author is successful, if he does "teach" us to look at "logs, rocks, and other large objects" differently, where will it end? What happens when, for "fun," they're all viewed as obstacles and race courses, when forests, prairies and mountains are turned into amusement parks? "Cycling" was synonymous with "low impact," "environmentally pure," and "socially conscious." Once touted as a "pollution solution" and an "answer to the Arabs," those days of delicate hopes seem to have gone the way of oil embargoes. But both will be back. And meanwhile hikers, thoughtful bikers and the public will begin considering the ban of mountain bikes from *all* lands. What a shame.

So much for where you *can't* ride. Your bike shop dealer will probably know of those nearby national and state parks and forests which—in addition to their "on-limits" roads—do have specific bike paths. And then there are the countless miles of paved and dirt roads, "multiple-use" forest land, backwoods lumber roads and fire trails. Don't make yourself miserable by concentrating on the few areas which exclude mountain bikes. Especially when it will take a lifetime to ride the areas which *are* open.

And now to the other matters you should consider before hitting the trail.

Riding Skills

Younger riders who have grown up bunny hopping over curbs on BMX bikes will have few problems avoiding trees and rocks on trails. But others should go easily at first. Begin by getting to know your bike on pavement, learning brake strength and gearing where you can concentrate on those things alone. Graduate to hard-packed dirt roads next, where you can practice moving in and out of ruts while avoiding rocks and tree limbs. Take on the grass shoulders of such roads next, or the clumps of scrub in desert areas. But remember, of course, what you'll already know if you ride a touring bike; shoulders attract glass and metal debris. (Although it increases rolling weight, I ride with tire liners—thin, tough belts of plastic which sit between the tube and tire. In all my desert riding through cactus thorns and commuting through nails and glass, I've had only one flat on a liner-equipped ATB tire.)

Learn the techniques of trail riding while on the easier dirt roads. Practice lifting the front wheel over objects in your path by pulling up on the handlebars as you shift your weight rearward by leaning back with the upper torso, and time this with a strong downstroke on the pedals. Shifting one's weight in the saddle is an important part of off-road cycling, and you'll have to spend a lot of time learning where weight should be on particular maneuvers—forward when the rear wheel is coming off a ledge or rock, rearward when traction is needed going up a hill, to the right or left side in an instant when you feel the bike slipping away on wet grass.

When you become proficient in all those moves you can try the "bunny hop" in which both wheels are off the ground at the same time to clear an obstacle. This is accomplished by lifting the handlebars (as above) while moving fairly fast; stop pedalling, and once in the air with the front tire shift your weight rapidly forward. Like derailleurs, there's no reason it should work—but it does.

Upper body strength is of great importance in trail riding and all-terrain touring. Whereas one develops it naturally while handling a bike (*especially* a loaded bike) off-road, very arduous rides will be enjoyed far more if one trains *before* hitting the trail. All forms of exercise will help, of course. I've lifted weights for years, switched off to isometrics at times, and isolated specific muscle groups with hand and chest mechanical exercisers. But the best of all training systems—

and the most pleasurable by far—is the rowing machine.

I prepared for my second Arizona tour on a Precor "612"—a tough, durable dual-piston workhorse which burns calories faster than cross-country skiing. The aerobic benefit is great, for major muscle groupings in the legs, arms, shoulders, stomach and back are employed. Rowing machines actually exercise more of the body than do stationary bikes, and are excellent devices to insure proper stretching. (Their near-silent operation and upright wall storage also make them the perfect foul weather/small space exerciser.)

Repairs

Horrible thought, isn't it? Easier not to think about it at all, to trust your luck and go for broke. But remember we're talking about *trail* riding in this section; try to hitch out of the backcountry after a breakdown and you'll change your mind about the hassles of being prepared. Sure tools are heavy, and represent another expense. But they'll last forever and cost only a fraction of what you'd spend on repair work done in bike shops. Besides, you already have this manual; with it, the correct tools, and some patience you've got all you need to become your own mechanic.

To know which tools to carry you have to know what to expect in breakdowns on the trail. (To know *how* to make the repairs simply refer to Part Two.) Off-road riding hazards and normal wear and tear can bring on the following problems.

1. *flats:* "liners" (like Mr. Tuffy) are a great preventative, as they shield that portion of the tube closest to the road surface. This is of course where thorns, nails, glass, et cetera work their way through the tread. But it *is* possible to catch a thorn in the unprotected sidewall. Necessary tools:

6 inch crescent wrench (to remove wheel axle nuts)

2 tire irons (for tire removal/replacement)

1 replacement tube and/or tube patch kit

air pump (Buy a good one—like a Zefal "HP"—and make sure it works *before* you need it. Also you'll probably need the kind that fits Schrader valves. That's the same valve that car tires use; many racing and touring bikes now come equipped with the smaller Presta valves. Know which one you're buying.)

tire pressure gauge (I don't carry one for trail riding for two reasons: precise air pressure isn't all that critical off-road, and I've gotten pretty good at gauging pressure by a squeeze. If you're a beginner you might take one along.)

2. broken gear/brake cable: the brake cables which come standard on most models are twice the thickness of those on touring bikes. Nevertheless, replacement cables are a must.

Necessary tools:

allen wrenches (Several brands of mountain bikes are equipped in such a way that allen wrenches of various sizes are all that's needed for many repairs or adjustments—handlebar and pedal removal, seat adjustment, cable replacement, etc. Be sure to have *all* the necessary sizes with you.)

replacement cables (one of each)

screwdriver/crescent wrench (If your bike requires these rather than an allen for cable replacement; study the attachment points on derailleurs, shifters, brakes and brake handles to determine what is necessary.)

small needle nose pliers with side-cutter (Useful for guiding cable during replacement, and cutting them to length. My derailleurs do not require the use of pliers, and I merely wrap the excess length until I'm home. In this way I avoid the weight while trail riding.)

3. broken spoke: hitting a rock or catching a limb with the wheel is always possible. Just pray it's the *front* wheel, for then it's so much simpler a repair (though a far worse fall).

Necessary tools:

6 inch crescent wrench

2 tire irons

spoke nipple wrench (be sure you have the correct size)

freewheel removal tool (there are many kinds available; check the name on your freewheel or ask your dealer).

SunTour Pocket Vise (This small tool is a dandy, for it takes the place of a full size vise or fifteen inch crescent in removing a frozen freewheel. Somewhat harder to use with a mountain bike's non-quick release wheels, the Pocket Vise can still mean the difference between walking or riding home.)

spokes (of the correct length and gauge. Buy extras when you purchase your bike; your dealer will know the ones you need. You'll find that the nipples will gradually back off the spare spokes due to road shock if they aren't taped in place. I always carry six spares taped securely to a chainstay or down tube, for otherwise they poke holes in panniers or get left behind.)

4. broken or frozen chain link: I was once on a ride in the San Juan Islands when a friend's chain snapped. He stood there muttering

"That's *never* happened to me before." An understandable sentiment, it nevertheless does nothing to get you on your way again. Be prepared for those breakdowns which can stop you cold; after that it's a trade-off between the weight of additional tools, and putting up with mechanical problems which are troublesome, but still rideable. (In that category are cone wrenches for wheel wobble, cotterless crank tools for loose chainrings, extra brake pads and shoes in case of loss....)
Necessary tools:
chain rivet tool (for removal/replacement of links, and freeing of frozen links)
5 extra chain links (be sure they will fit your chain, for links come in different sizes)

5. *loose headset:* the jaws of a six inch crescent wrench aren't quite large enough for this task.
Necessary tool:
7 inch channel locks (This handy tool also performs a host of other jobs on the bike, and doubles as a pot grip around the campfire.)

6. *derailleur out of adjustment:* this can happen at any time, and fine tuning is of course necessary after cable replacement.
Necessary tool:
regular blade screwdriver (The one I carry has an overall length of about six inches, and a flat blade tip only 3/16" wide. Buy a good one and the tip won't bend or begin to flake after a few hard turns.)

Beyond tools and other items mentioned above are those accessories which should accompany you for safety and/or comfort.

Non-medical trail accessories
1. *rack bolts* (These are the small allen head bolts which attach the luggage racks to the frame. Break or lose one of these without a replacement and you're in trouble. Make sure the bolt's threads match your frame fittings, and that you have the allen wrench which fits.)
2. *water bottles* (On one particularly brutal desert ride I mounted eight bottle holders on my frame, and still had to carry canteens in my panniers. The extra weight is no fun, but dehydration is worse.)
3. *sunglasses* (You'd take a pair on any ride, but these are especially important when on backwoods roads and trails. Branches seem to come from nowhere when you're concerned with staying in the saddle over rough terrain, and thus your eyes have *got* to have protection. I've tried the lightweight models with plastic lenses, and find that they are

scratched far too easily. More recently I've used the Bausch and Lomb "Ambermatics"—so that I can wear them no matter how overcast the day—with glass lenses, wrap-around ear construction and a hard, belt-mounted case. And while they cost more than you'd probably prefer to pay, they're like bikes in this respect: quality requires buying only once.)

4. *rain gear* (A simple poncho will do for most trail riding, if it's warm weather and a one-day ride. For extended trail rides you should consider the optional suits and accessory wear discussed in Chapter Four.)

5. *knife* (I've packed the same Swiss Army knife for a decade. Sure they're expensive, but they're also precision tools with a hundred uses and a century of life. My ever-present Buck Esquire 501 pocketknife accompanies me on trails.)

Medical trail accessories

A full complement of medical supplies is suggested in Chapter Five, but you should carry at least the following items to staunch blood flow and deal with rattlesnake or copperhead attack.

1. *snakebite kit* (Read the instructions *before* you're bitten.)

2. *bandaids*

3. *gauze compress pads* (I carry a half-dozen of the 4" x 4" size, plus an Army combat bandage—available at government surplus stores. This will appear to be overkill until you've seen what the combination of slickrock and injudicious riding can do. For that matter, most biker's wounds incurred upon leaving the saddle bring on large surface area scrapes. Slide along on pavement or rock or gravel and you'll require more than a few bandaids to patch you up.)

4. *gauze* (1 roll, 2" x 20 yards; can be used instead of tape to hold compress pads in place, and instead of bandaids when perspiration causes them to peel off)

5. *ace bandages* (I carry two for minor sprains.)

6. *moleskin* (This is great *before* a blister, but once one forms try a new product by Spenco called "2nd Skin Dressing." It's amazingly effective in ending pain and friction, but must be held in place by tape, gauze, or a special moleskin-like "Adhesive Knit" which comes with the "2nd Skin." I've only used it thus far on blisters, but it's suggested for rashes, burns, abrasions and stings.)

7. *iodine* (Small plastic bottle for the tiny nicks and cuts lurking along the trail.)

8. *Benadryl* (This prescription antihistamine is used by those who have highly allergic reactions to some plants, insect bites, etc. Because I

tour alone so often, and especially when in areas of unfamiliar flora and fauna, I carry this in case of an unexpected reaction to something unfamiliar.)

Most of these items will never be needed, and because of their infrequent use are often forgotten when a person packs for the trail. I've solved this difficulty by placing all my medical supplies in a small yellow stuff sack, and forcing myself to look for it while I'm checking for my similar-sized tool bag. I also suggest that you prepare for medical problems in the same way the experts train people in self-defense; you won't go to pieces if you've already gone through it all in your mind. Try your best to imagine the blood and pain, and then ask yourself what you would do.

For example: some hotdog on a downhill trail flips off his bike. He lands on a fallen branch which snaps in two, and the sharp point catches him in the ribs. Now, every soldier learns to place the combat bandage plastic liner over holes in the chest, to prevent a collapsed lung. But how many civilians would know of this danger, or that a VISA card held in place over the hole can save a life? Go through each and every step, imagining the next problem and not leaving it until it's solved.

a) So you've extracted the branch, but you've never believed in credit and thus don't have a card . . .

b) Simple, you laminated your driver's license some time ago—

c) But how to hold it in place? The gauze?

d) No, for another cyclist is already using that on the patient's other wounds. What to do?

e) That's easy; you give the nearly comatose victim a short lesson in ethics, explaining that he must learn the consequences of his actions, that he can now hold the license in place or croak. If he's still conscious after that you move on into the realm of libertarian thought, stating that he surely has the *right* to die, but . . .

f) If you like the guy and have thought ahead, you tie the ace bandages together and wrap him, mummy-style, to hold the license in place.

Don't go through life kicking yourself because you made a bad decision, or couldn't think fast enough when time was short. If you've gone through it all before it happens, and have the first aid kit along, you'll do all right. (Look at the Madden "Cyclist Emergency Kit" as a great trail accompaniment.)

Packs and luggage racks

One final consideration in this chapter is how to carry the gear necessary for a full day of backcountry trail riding. You'll find a thorough discussion of mountain bike panniers in the appendix, but there are alternatives for very short trips. Trail riders can usually fit all they need in a single pannier, but wheels rebel when weight is carried on only one side. If you don't wish to divide that weight between two panniers then a single bag positioned directly over the front or rear wheel is the answer.

It's time for making choices once again. There are several kinds of handlebar bags (even one which can mount *behind* the saddle), bags which attach to the seat post, and bags designed to mount directly on top of the rear rack. Beyond location, they differ in mounting technique (and therefore in ease of removal and reattachment), in material, design, capacity, color and cost. The best way to make a wise choice of bags is to request a catalogue and price sheet from all the manufacturers (see appendix), visit bike shops to examine a few first-hand, and read the advertisements in biking magazines.

I will, however, mention a few I've tried and liked.

1. I've tested large handlebar bags on trail rides and found them unstable; the weight is also in the wrong place for lifting the front wheel. However, Eclipse makes a dandy two-ounce "Seat Post Thing" which enables the bag to be mounted in the rear. In testing this system I found that if the suspension straps are cinched tightly the bag is acceptably stable. For the person who already owns a full set of touring bags and doesn't wish to buy more for his ATB this alternative is hard to beat.

2. Small handlebar bags are fine on mountain bikes, although none of the brands I've tested are large enough by themselves to hold all that I carry while trail riding. Nevertheless, I've found the Lone Peak bag to be excellent in all respects except its lack of a map case, and in ease of removal. Neither of these points is important for most trail riders, but they are cause for concern if you decide to try all-terrain touring.

On tours I pack my wallet, passport, note pad and pen in my handlebar bag, and therefore like to take it with me for meals inside cafes. In addition, a map case is necessary for touring and even helps if you're trail riding with a topo map. The Kirtland "Compact Handlebar Bag," somewhat easier to remove and considerably smaller than the Lone Peak, does have a nice removable map case. As with our discussion of frames, we're again in the realm of trade-offs. I prefer the size of Lone Peak, but like the map case of the Kirtland. I know which factor is more important to me; you need to think it over and compare costs before deciding for yourself. I've used another system recently for trail riding and touring, the Specialized duo of "Tailwind Moose Bag" and

"Tailwind Large Saddle Stuffer." The first is an extremely durable handlebar bag with a three-point mounting system. However, unlike the Kirtland model, it employs a special locking cinch strap in place of velcro, producing a very stable ride. Capacity is less than Lone Peak, similar to Kirtland, and the bag does not have a map case. However, it *is* equipped with an easily accessible second pocket, perfect for sunglasses or anything the rider might wish to reach without stopping. This smaller pocket rests possum-like on the top of the larger, zippered pouch, and velcroes closed. (Handlebar bags require *dual* zippers for easy use while pedalling; unfortunately *none* I've tested are equipped thusly.) The second bag, the Saddle Stuffer, is velcroed and buckled ("Fastex" side-release) into place. Small and stable, this two-pocketed unobtrusive pack is a good location for the commuter's poncho. (Larger seat bags are available; Kangaroo also makes a handlebar bag.)

3. My first choice for trail riding is a "rack pack," a bag designed to ride on top of the rear carrier. Again there are many makes and models, but a real beauty I've tested is the Kirtland "Blazer Rack Pack." Its durable construction, heavy weight Cordura material, silver striping of Scotchlite "reflective trim" (for night visibility) and large capacity makes it ideal as both a trail and commuting bag. But its mounting system is its greatest attribute. Shaped like a loaf of bread, the pack rides lengthwise along the rack. The narrow end is secured with a strip of velcro, while two large web belts (sewn into—not just under—the bottom and side walls of the pack) slip around the top rack frame tube, then up and over the bag. In the old days a laborious web cinch would be required here, to connect the web belts from either side of the pack. Instead, light weight but extremely tough plastic Fastex buckles now snap closed or open in a second. The bag is off the bike in a moment, but will never *fall* off.

4. Another pack which deserves honorable mention here is the Lone Peak "Deluxe Eight Pack Rack Pack." It too employs Fastex buckles, and can be mounted faster than one can pronounce the bag's cumbersome name. A "waterproof insulated vinyl liner allows you to pour ice over your bottles or tall cans of your favorite beverage," an external mesh pocket completely around the pack can store a wallet or windbreaker, a sleeve is provided to hold a Citadel-type hoop lock, and a shoulder strap is provided. Ice cold drinks after a hot trail ride—it's like carrying a cooler in your trunk.

5. Although I'll speak later of panniers I should mention two brands here, for their special backpack features. During my desert ride in '83 to the Colorado River, especially on the thousand foot descent into the Gorge, I found the Madden mountain bike panniers invaluable. Mad-

den has designed a system wherein a huge top bag snaps into place over the rear wheel, attaching to both rear panniers. When the terrain or your fancy turns to walking, this top bag is unsnapped, two padded shoulder straps are slipped out of their hidden compartment, and a serviceable backpack is ready for work. Lone Peak now offers a "mountain bike backpack conversion." The system is quite different from Madden (the straps and backpack mount are separate from the bags). A very recent production, I've not yet tested it.

Now to racks. With many brands available you should take some time and decide for yourself which rack to buy. But allow me two personal comments.

1. I believe there's no stiffer, stronger rack around than those made by Bruce Gordon. Constructed of 4130 chrome-moly, it's like riding with a rack that's part of—not an addition to—the frame. Gordon racks are designed to provide a custom fit with the equally excellent Needle Works panniers. Both must be mail-ordered (address in appendix).

2. I'd like to suggest that the industry is making a mistake in equipping ATBs with low-riders (low-riding front racks). The argument of increased stability due to the lower position of the weight makes sense on touring bikes, but is of minimal importance on bikes which are already so inherently stable due to larger tire, rim and frame tube size. But that isn't really the point. The difficulty is that to gain the slight increase in stability the bags are placed in exactly the position *most* likely to cause problems—low to the ground, and therefore close to obstacles along the trail.

I've tested this idea in the field, over all kinds of terrain, by making sure either my companion's bike or mine was set up with low-riders. The second bike was equipped with the normal-height front rack. On every trail ride through very rough country—thick sage or Midwest undergrowth, along gullies and creeks, and through rock-strewn fields— the panniers riding low to the ground took a real beating. I was myself once wedged between two rocks in New Mexico, unable to follow a high-rack bike through a narrow gap in the sandstone. And a further problem is created by branches which can become stuck in the vertical webbing present on some front panniers.

Well. You ought to be ready for the trail. Ride where it's legal, take your tools and first aid kit, and avoid headplants.

CHAPTER FOUR

COMMUTING ON AN ATB

When I wrote my first book a few years ago the cost per driven mile for a compact car was approximately 38¢. Americans then, as now, drove on average about ten thousand miles per year. The annual operating expense came to a whopping $3800.

In 1984 that per mile cost was 44¢; the annual expense $4400. For a compact. For normalcy. For admission into that wonderful twice-a-day game of "rush hour."

In the Foreword of that earlier book I argued that it made little sense to spend one's time fighting traffic to and from work, and then take more time to jog. The aerobic benefit of cycling is nearly as great, I counseled, and biking is far better for one's health overall. In chapter after chapter I explained how I solved the problems of traffic, inclement weather, fears for personal safety, night riding, and how to dress for both the road and work, or pack a change of unwrinkled clothes.

The reasons for cycling—and especially for cycling to and from work—are still the same. Except that now one saves even *more* money by doing so. And, more importantly, the development of the ATB has made commuting easier and much safer.

It's easier because the extremely low gearing allows you to take the steepest hills and stiffest winds without working hard. It's safer because the bikes are so inherently stable, because thumb-shifters allow one's hands to remain on the handlebars, and because the wide tires can cross sewer gratings without falling in. The upright riding position reduces the chance of headplants, enormous brakes stop you in an instant, and huge pedals allow sure footing without the worries of toe clips and straps. And, most important of all, the bike's durability and light weight allow you to hop curbs at will, thereby escaping traffic altogether. Gone are the fears that gravel, glass or sand along the shoulder will bring on a fall, or that chuckholes will collapse a wheel.

The ease and safety of travel, the avoidance of adding one's own entry to the daily race of rush hour; how is it that people yet prefer the motorized, metal box to mountain bikes? Perhaps it's that initial cost. A car's expense is so spread out in time payments and gas and license fees. Penury by installment seems less distasteful. Contrast that—the hidden fees—with the way one buys an ATB. It's all up front. Most shops demand payment in full, and that's a lot of bread to drop at once.

But look at it this way. Commute by bike for three or four months— a bit longer if you live less than five miles from work, a much shorter time if your car is bigger than a compact—and the money saved will buy your mountain bike. What a deal.

I've discussed commuting by bike in detail in other books and articles, and will therefore run quickly through a checklist of the necessary gear. I'll also provide information on mechanical changes which will make your travel more efficient, and a few techniques to lessen the likelihood of theft. Finally, I'll comment on those relatively new products which I've tested recently and found to be advantageous to commuters.

Equipping the commuter bike

1. *tires:* New mountain bike tires are coming out all the time for road, trail, and city riding. These wide choices are made possible by a rim size (26 x 1.75) which will accept tires of greatly differing widths. Everything from a narrow profile tire only 1.5″ wide to the huge knobbies of 2.125″ is available.

TIRE PROFILES

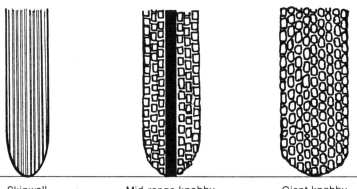

Skinwall   Mid-range knobby   Giant knobby

In Chapter Two I discussed the benefits of alloy wheels (in place of steel) and skinwall tires (instead of gum). The reduction in rolling weight was explained, and I therefore assume you understand why—under the commuting conditions of good road surface, long distance, and a desire for the fastest ride—many cyclists will choose the skinwall 1.5″ tire. With tire liners one should ride these radials for years without a flat.

But there are sacrifices in such a system. The ride is harsher, the bike handles chuckholes and rough pavement far less forgivingly, and one cannot hop curbs or run across sewer gratings with abandon. A slightly larger tire—the 1.75″—is in my estimation a better compromise. But it still requires greater attention to riding style than I wish to give.

My preference for all but the two extremes—very long commuting distances on good roads and in good weather, or terrible road surfaces and travel in snow—is the 26 x 2.10, with knobby sides and a raised center bead of rubber. I've found that I can commute with this set-up through three seasons, handle every hazard and curb that comes my way, and still ride with good speed. In addition, I don't have to change tires for weekend dirt road and off-road runs, unless I'm pedalling extremely soft surfaces.

You may not think there's much to the fractional difference between the 2.10″ and the giant knobby 2.125″ (which takes on *everything* successfully, except loose sand). But there is. I've ridden for a year on the excellent Carlisle Aggressor Road/Trail tires, rated at 65 psi (most knobbies are rated at 35-40 psi). At this pressure and on pavement the tire zips along with only the road contact of the very narrow center rubber bead. On tight turns, or once in dirt or gravel, the tire sinks to its knobby sides and gains the traction necessary for stability. The 2.10″ uses the smaller, lighter 1.75″ tube, and, when of skinwall construction and equipped with a liner, is a lightweight workhorse that can't be topped.

And then there's snow. Those great mornings when before dawn you peer outside to count the inches, and see huge white flakes falling by the thousands from a black sky. Do you warm the engine, shovel the driveway, and spend an *extra* hour in the slush and rush to work? Or *ride* the snow-filled sidewalks and backstreets instead? Let yourself recapture the excitement of such days when as a kid you watched those flakes pile up. The 2.125″ knobbies will handle the snow, and you'll get to work feeling like you've pedalled a bobsled.

2. *fenders:* Several companies now make fenders for ATBs. They're heavy—the Bluemels I ride with weigh nineteen ounces—but they're

extremely tough. For commuting there's no choice but to mount a pair, unless you plan never to ride through puddles, mud, or in the rain. You'll also find they protect far more than just your clothes; brakes, rack packs and your front derailleur are all spared the road grime which is picked up when streets are wet.

I also ride trails with my Bluemels, and have found their durability sufficient for the hard knocks they receive. The majority of their weight comes in the mounting hardware, particularly the fender stays; you won't begrudge them the extra ounces when you see how they perform. One suggestion: add a drop of Loc-Tight on each fender stay mounting screw.

Concerning fender size, Bluemel makes a three-quarter length "Mountain Range" which fits the 2.125″ tire, and a full-length "City" series for widths up to 1.75″. The wider "Mountain Range" is preferable for muddy trail riding, as less buildup results with a shorter fender. And the thinner, longer "City" is necessary to keep road water from spraying onto the rider's back. But there's a problem; what happens on those snowy days when a commuter *needs* the wider tire? And who wants the hassle of changing fenders all the time?

An answer for non-trail riders is the well made, full-length, wider ESGE fenders (available in chrome *and* a snazzy "smoke"). But for those who ride everywhere a second choice is a large, homemade mudflap (fashioned from a plastic milk carton), attached by a small bolt to the "Mountain Range"; this can be removed for muddy weekend trails. Fender companies should offer such an option as standard fare.

3. *gearing changes:* I explained in Chapter Two why it is important to have a low range in the mid-20s, and promised to discuss extending the high-end range as well. Personally, I find this to be necessary for commuting and touring; otherwise I coast a lot. But the problem is that most bikes come equipped with a largest chainring of 46 teeth; when used in conjunction with the smallest freewheel cog of 14 teeth a gear of only 85.4 inches is attained (see gear chart in Appendix). That's plenty on the trail, in soft surfaces with low pressure tires. But center rib tires on city streets reduce that rolling resistance drastically, and a higher gear is needed to take advantage of this speed.

Some ATBs come equipped with a largest chainring of 48 teeth, which gives a high gear of 89.1 on a 14 tooth freewheel cog. That's better. But it's not *that* much better. Instead, I suggest dropping that smallest freewheel cog to a 13. With a chainring of 48 teeth it will jump your high-end gear to a very respectable 96. From a mid-20s low to nearly 100 high—now *that's* a range. (Ask your dealer if it's too much range for your derailleur; the term is "chain wrapping ability.")

Unfortunately, not all freewheels will accept 13 tooth cogs. Ask your dealer at the time of purchase if your freewheel will accept the change; he'll probably replace it for a nominal fee, or you can do it later by yourself. I know. If you're new at this the very *idea* of changing freewheel cogs is anathema to mental health. But don't worry. Read over the instructions in Part Two, and give it a try.

4. *racks:* I've discussed racks in Chapter Three, suggesting the avoidance of low-riders on trails. While I prefer the normal height rack for commuting as well, for it provides another carrying surface for packs and other gear, the low-riders obviously do *not* have the same drawbacks in the city.

5. *packs:* Begin your search for the perfect commuting bag by reading my remarks on rack packs in Chapter Three, and on panniers in Chapter Five. Next, take into consideration your geographic region, riding distance, and clothing on the job. For example, an office worker in Seattle with a roundtrip of fifteen miles will have to have the carrying capacity for rain gear and sport coat, slacks, skirt.... But no such problems exist, of course, for those who live three miles from work in Florida.

Contrary to popular belief, one does *not* require a shower after pedalling short distances. On hot days a biker will usually choose shorts and a T-shirt for the ride to work. A washcloth is packed along for a quick rinse of the upper torso at a bathroom sink, then fresh deodorant and a shirt is donned, slacks slipped on, and one is ready for the desk or shop. I've found over the last decade without a car that only during summer months is it necessary for me to take a change of undershirts. After a while you'll learn to press easily up the hills, and slow down for the last three blocks or so, to prevent buildup of perspiration.

You'll also learn the principle of "layering" in dress; gone are bulky, heavy car coats and parkas, and thick cotton longjohns which feel clammy when worn while exercising. They're replaced by thin polypropylene underwear (*fantastic* at wicking away moisture from one's skin), a shirt and well-ventilated jacket. Too warm? The lightweight jacket is opened or removed. Too cold? A sweater vest is donned. The principle is simple: dress in layers so as to alter your clothing as your body's thermal requirements change.

But back to packs. A single, small commuting bag is one possibility; in this is placed the tools, first aid kit, poncho and other road accessories you'll need with you always. All other needs: jacket, change of clothes, further rainwear or cold weather gear, lunch, etc. are packed in a single pannier. An obvious alternative is to divide one's kit of "necessaries" between two panniers, thereby assuring yourself adequate space for other gear, and the mandatory balance of weight on both sides of the wheel. But there's a problem in that choice: the hassle of pannier removal and attachment each time you stop.

Eclipse has a solution. Almost a year ago the company sent me their "Commuter Baskets" for testing. Available in either a "slide mount" (for Eclipse racks and brackets) or "clamp on" system (adaptable to all racks), the packs are constructed of tough nylon knitting, cordura panels and aircraft grade aluminum. Sized perfectly for a grocery bag, the basket folds to a 1½" width when not in use, and snaps closed. The beauty of this arrangement is two-fold; first, any item or other bag or briefcase can be tossed into the deep baskets and carried with ease; second, with the "slide mount" system—in which the baskets are secured to the rack with screws—one feels reasonably safe in leaving them while away from the bike. This second advantage can be gained with any rack by ordering the baskets in the "slide mount" style, and buying an accessory "bolt-on adaptor" (for use with Blackburn-type racks) or a "strap-on adaptor" (for use with all racks). My preference is the bolt-on, as the strap-on slides about at times.

I find these baskets so handy that they've been off my bike only when I'm on tour, and when testing other products. For me they're the perfect commuting option. If, however, you prefer bags to brackets, and still want a system which is easily removed, I suggest you look at the Eclipse "Nomad Commuter" panniers. These are permanently joined, and are simply draped over any luggage rack. Velcro strips on the Nomad underside engage the velcro which one wraps around the rack, and two more velcro strips which are sewn to the panniers are then wrapped around the seat stays. Quick and simple, with 1150 cubic inches of space. These bags have a convenient center handle for carrying while off the bike, and may be suspended from a shoulder strap. (Look at Kirtland's "Courier" and "Commuter" series also.)

Finally, a word on briefcase panniers. Three companies have sent theirs for testing—Madden, Kirtland and Lone Peak. All are extremely well made, and mount easily and securely to bikes without cantilever brakes. However, the spacing of their attachment clamps or hooks, and the rearward mounting position required by the cantilevers, prohibits use of the Kirtland and Lone Peak briefcases on ATBs with cantilevers; the Madden just does fit on the rack. Now, it is very possible that Kirtland and Lone Peak will have adapted their mount system by the time you read this, especially since so many touring bikes are now equipped with cantilevers. Or you can do as I have for a year, and merely toss *any* of the three cases into an Eclipse basket for the ride.

But let me say another word about these bags. All three are appropriate for the businessman, with separate dividers and compartments for papers, pens and calculators. They're dressy, too; lawyers needn't feel a bit self-conscious in judge's chambers with these bags in their hands. Yet their slim, sleek design is a drawback for the student, who needs the room to carry several books and notebooks, plus a lunch.

The Madden "Caravelle" briefcase, with a width of four inches, is about twice as deep as Kirtland and Lone Peak. But my choice for the college-bound (and something I've used as my commuting bag as well) is the Madden "Omni." This is actually a briefcase/day pack pannier set, which when off the bike can be zipped together easily and carried by its handle or a shoulder strap. Hands full? No problem for this versatile company (see remarks on other Madden panniers in Chapters Three and Five); padded shoulder straps appear from a zipped, concealed compartment.

So if you pack a lot of gear and want the shortest set-up time before you're in the saddle, try this: Eclipse "Commuter Baskets" and the Madden "Omni" pair. A bag in each basket balances the load, and once at your plant or school or office the packs are zipped together for ease in carrying.

I almost forgot the rain. More and more packs these days are billed as "waterproof," but moisture has a way of getting under the rain flaps, through the zippers, and onto items you *don't* want wet. I choose to be sure by buying pannier "rain covers," and slipping them in place at the first drop. (A plastic bag does the trick with items inside baskets.)

6. *lights/reflectors:* It's a shame. Just when the industry got around to making the mountain bike—the perfect commuting bicycle—it developed a fine little chainstay-mount generator light which doesn't fit on ATBs with fenders. The lights are great. No more would poorly mounted fork and seatstay generators flip into one's spokes, or eat up a sidewall. And the krypton bulbs now used are far brighter than those of old (and are claimed to be more durable than halogens). Two wonderful developments for riding around town, but they're incompatible. Why?

First, there's the difficulty of chainstay width. Wide mountain bike tires require a chainstay width too great for the generator mounting bracket. And while one would expect this problem to be soon alleviated by the lighting manufacturers of Sanyo and Soubitez, the second problem is more critical: how can a generator wheel run smoothly on a knobby tire surface?

Of course they'll work if the tire has a raised center bead (in which case you can mount your generator to the brake bridge—but *not* if you have fenders). Yet that still leaves you lightless during winter, when the big knobbies are required. So much for progess; we're back to batteries. And here, I'm afraid, is where I'll have to leave you on your own, for the options are far too numerous to list. There are handlebar mounted flashlight holders, quick-release "Cat Eye" lights, and lights which run on "Ni-Cd" batteries. The problem with most battery lights is that while they do enable motorists to see *you*, their puny beams barely stretch out to the front end of your rack. Some companies claim wonderful results with their nickel-cadmium rechargeable battery lights, but conversations with several discerning owners indicate that such systems still leave a lot to be desired. And they aren't inexpensive.

While headlights are therefore still a problem (until the generator lighting companies change their chainstay brackets, and even then if you're riding knobbies), we have no such trouble with lighting in the rear. And this is understandable, for the goal there is merely to be seen. Generators usually sport red tail lights, and large constant-beam battery lights are also available. But the tail light I like most of all is the "Belt Beacon," a large, flashing amber light with an extremely strong belt clip. It comes in either a forty or sixty flash per minute model, and runs on a single nine volt transistor radio-type battery. Extremely durable, it has never failed me—even in the hardest rains. And because the light isn't continuous the battery lasts a long, long time. (Mine receives much use, and has had the same battery for almost a year.)

Yet no matter how new your batteries or your brand of light, something can always go wrong. You can make it home with street lights by riding slowly, or buy a flashlight at a store, or push your bike if it's totally dark. But these are times when it's more important to *be* seen, and this is when reflectors are a *must*. Required by law in the rear (a headlight is required in front), they're also a good idea in front, and a great idea in the pedals where the movement makes them particularly effective in attracting attention.

I usually avoid front fork generators, for fear of road shock throwing the light into the spokes. (This is bad enough on the rear wheel, but if anything attacks one's front spokes a headplant results.) However, Daryl Schueller—a friend in St. Louis—spent this past winter experimenting with lighting for his mountain bike. While he found that seatstay-mounted generators wouldn't work, he did come up with the following system: a Soubitez front fork generator (the metal contact wheel resting on the tire sidewall *just* below the knobs), a back-up Cat Eye battery light on the handlebars, and a "Belt Beacon" in rear.

7. *horns and handlebar bells:* Lights let people see you, but sometimes it's important to be *heard*. I ride with a handlebar bell, a most civilized appeal to people to take notice. This is especially effective with pedestrians, who often think I'm an ice cream truck. When the weather's warm and windows are down many motorists will also hear you. But in winter, or when the traffic's loud and fast, I'm forced to bellow. Surprisingly, it works most every time.

If you're really out for noise you'll be delighted with a piercing screamer called "Super Sound." Painfully loud, it's emitted from a tiny can of compressed air, and can be carried in a small holder on your handlebars. For years I've suggested this for women who ride alone or at night, as it awakens neighborhoods in an instant.

8. *seat post bolt:* Quick-release bolts on mountain bike seat posts are great for trail and touring. But try commuting in my town with it and you'll soon be riding standing up. Face it. It's just too tempting for a thief.

Instead, ask for a two inch long 6mm bolt from the hardware store. Buy a lock washer and two nuts as well, and replace your quick release with it. I also use the non-threaded serrated washer which comes on the quick-release; this I place on the bolt head side of the seat tube, leaving the lock washer and both nuts for the other side. My hope (thus far it's worked) is that a thief won't take the time to struggle with the nuts.

9. *locks:* Citadel. Or a hoop lock of another name—like Kryptonite. Use a cable—any cable— and you're going to lose your bike. I know hoop locks are heavy and expensive, but I always carry two (the second is for the front wheel).

But where should they be carried? Special frame-mounted holders are now available, and some "rack packs" have built-in sleeves to hold a single lock. But my solution is simple, inexpensive, and even more convenient. I employ two large hose clamps (available at hardware and auto shops), attaching them to the seat bag slots present on many saddles. A single lock can hang from these clamps (the weight of two can rip the slot); on larger frames it will hang about two inches above the rack, and will not swing about enough while riding to be felt. If your saddle height puts the lock closer to the rack, use a bungie to hold it in place. (I normally toss my second lock into my Eclipse Commuter basket, but another solution allows *both* locks to be suspended from the saddle. At your local hardware store you'll find "plastic ties" or "plastic bundling straps"—two of the many names for this product. Purchase two eight inch long straps, thread them through the seat bag slot, then around the metal saddle support rail, and lock the tie in place. The heavy gauge plastic will retain its shape, making it easy to slip the locks in and out.)

10. *mirror:* I simply can't believe I rode so long without one. Now, of course, there are all kinds; little dental mirrors which wrap around one's glasses, mirrors which velcro to a wrist, and others with convex glass and bar-end mounts.

I've tried two on my ATB. I began my Southwest tour with the "Art-Form" mirror. This well-made accessory takes the place of one's bar-end plug, and does its job without vibration. But a nasty fall of the bike (when I wasn't on it—a large black dog was eating my water bottle) broke it into several pieces. The problem with this mirror is that there's no way in which to turn the glass so as to avoid contact with the ground in case of fall. And so the search was on.

The answer came from a well-stocked bike shop in Santa Fe. Light in weight and cost, the Cat Eye "Model BMG" has a bar-end mount, and is made so that the mirror can be turned away from any possible contact with the ground.

11. *safety flag:* You know how visible these flags are. How many times have you seen that orange pennant flapping about a hundred yards ahead on the road, or above the height of traffic? As with pedal reflectors, the bright color *and* movement combine to grab the motorist's eye.

I prefer the single piece, stiff fiberglass rod, mounted off the front left axle and restrained from moving toward the rider's face by the front rack. In this location it's handy for use as a whip, should some charging dog or other beast require it. (However, if your commute includes a lot of sidewalk riding beneath low-hanging branches, I'd leave it at home.)

12. *kickstand:* The ATBs' "bull-moose" handlebars make them slightly more difficult than touring bikes to lean against buildings. There's also the problem of bikes rolling forward or backward if bumped by a passerby while you're away. (The "Flickstand" device is usually suggested to deal with this difficulty; unfortunately, commuting bikes have fenders which render Flickstands ineffective.) Thus the ease and convenience of a lightweight, aluminum kickstand is even more pronounced than on touring bikes.

13. *water bottle:* Most commuting distances do not require water along the way, but I always pack a bottle filled with another liquid:

straight ammonia—my second line of defense against dogs. Perhaps not as easy to use as "Halt" (the aerosol repellent) on animals, or tear gas against man, it nevertheless is unaffected by cold, is less expensive, and isn't perceived by the assailant—until too late—as a means of defense. (Some aerosols won't work at temperatures below 20° F.)

14. *air pump:* I mentioned the Zefal "HP" in Chapter Three; here I want only to add a reminder not to leave it on your bike. In fact, I find that even when securely mounted the pump can be jarred loose while hopping curbs. I prefer to carry everything (except the water bottle of ammonia) which I'm not leaving on my bike in a single bag; in this way I simply lock the bike at the end of my ride, grab the bag and bottle, and I'm finished. Otherwise, the temptation is great to leave the pump "for just a second" while in a store on the way home.

15. *bike cart:* So it's someone's birthday and you want to take a cake to work, or need to carry something larger than a pannier. Sure you can drive, but there's another alternative: pack it along in a light, weather-tight cart which has eight thousand cubic inches of space, and is made to wheel through standard doorways with a half-inch to spare. For the past year I've been testing the CycleTote "Tour" trailer, and have found that its welded, tubular aluminum frame and "No Roll" safety hitch make for a fast, safe, untroubled ride. (address in Appendix)

16. *pedals:* In Chapter Three I discussed the requirements of good mountain bike pedals, and stated that clips are made even for the huge bear-traps. But the secure grip provided by the rat trap edge, and the freedom of not having to worry about slipping into clips and straps again after each stop, has made me decide against attaching clips for commuting. There is one noticeable drawback, however; while strad-dling the bike and waiting for a break in traffic, with the pedal in the six o'clock position, one cannot just raise a foot and expect the crankarm to follow. Instead, I have to draw the pedal up with the toe of my shoe before I start to ride. This was extremely bothersome to me at first, especially because I'd ridden only clips and straps for fifteen years. But within two weeks I was used to pedals alone and now ride clips only when touring on my ATB.

Another nice thing about bear-trap pedals is that the very good ones are so large that almost any shoe will work—especially if assisted by another Spenco product, "Orthotic Arch Supports." I've even tried out tennis shoes on my touring bike with these supports and found they work very well.

17. *rainwear:* During warm weather a poncho is the answer for staying dry. In testing a few of the Gore-tex suits I've found them better than conventional wear at passing moisture away from a body, but not sufficiently effective to justify the cost. My preference is a poncho, chaps and rain boots for the warmer months, and a rainsuit like the one by Cannondale when cold.

The Cannondale suit is one hundred per cent lightweight nylon; the jacket has a large air flap at the back, and zippered air vents under both arms. Completely washable, the suit takes up little space in a pannier. Eclipse sells a very good poncho of nylon taffeta, waterproofed with "Super K-Kote" and double seamed throughout. (K-Kote products, after hard use, sometimes lose their ability to repel water. This can be remedied by a simple application of K-Kote, available in cans through mail-order and specialty sports shops.) Burley makes a somewhat heavier "rain cape," and is one of only a few companies offering shoe covers (rain boots which require seam sealing and leak somewhat even then). For the wet *and* cold days you might look at the Needle Works "Hotfoots"; thinsulate inside, a nylon oxford lining, and eleven-ounce Cordura soles.

18. *cold weather gear:* While it's true that cycling will keep you surprisingly warm on very cold days, there are still those bone-chilling morning rides in winter when your body needs all the insulation it can get. Don't forget the principle of layering. Begin with polypropylene (it comes in different thicknesses; I use the lightest weight for commuting) and work out from there. Bodies lose a great deal of heat through the head if it's uncovered, and fingers and toes will often be the first to yell if you're not dressed correctly. My choices have evolved to stocking caps, polypropylene liners and wool blend socks, and huge Grandoe ski gloves.

But that still leaves the face. My beard helps, but for the worst of wind-chill days I now employ the "Masque." Produced by Edwards Ski Products of Salt Lake, it covers only nose, cheeks, chin and ears, and velcroes snugly behind the neck. I've found this system far preferable to pull-over masks. And unlike those made of cloth, the neoprene "Masque" doesn't become frozen around one's mouth.

Kangaroo makes an excellent jacket for commuting and touring. Constructed of Gore-tex and polypropylene, it has a high neck, long sleeves (so that wrists aren't exposed while arms are outstretched on the handlebars) and three pockets across the back.

Commuter's Checklist

You'll develop your own list after several weeks of riding, tailored to fit your particular commuting conditions—climate, distance to work, road conditions.... I provide the following merely as a guide from which to begin. (Review those items discussed above for suggestions of on-bike equipment.)

Tools:

1. 6 inch crescent wrench
2. regular blade screwdriver
3. needle-nose pliers
4. channel locks
5. tire levers
6. allen wrenches
7. cone wrenches
8. chain rivet tool
9. spoke wrench
10. freewheel tool
11. Suntour Pocket Vise

Medical:

1. bandaids
2. gauze compress pads
3. gauze
4. ace bandages
5. iodine

Miscellaneous:

1. brake/gear cable
2. tube/tube patch kit
3. extra chain links
4. air pump
5. air gauge
6. extra spokes
7. water (ammonia) bottle
8. headlight/tail light
9. rain gear
10. sunglasses/goggles
11. pants clips
12. bungie (shock cord)

CHAPTER FIVE
ALL-TERRAIN TOURING

I made my case for this new concept of touring in Chapter One when I mentioned the freedom from people and cars, and the opening of quiet miles previously unapproachable for cyclists. I alluded to the benefits derived from riding backwoods trails and dirt roads through the hinterlands, while retaining the ability to travel fast on pavement. And I spoke of it as compromise, that halfway world between the senses-numbing weight of backpacks, and the highway noise of autos at one's elbow.

Yet as in all attempts to strike a balance, some things are given up. You can't expect to cover as much ground each day as with a touring bike, or find the trails as easy to negotiate when you're loaded down with gear. Instead, you'll discover that which is gained simply by slowing down and learning to *observe*.

In this last chapter before we turn to mechanics I want to show you, by example, how different a tour can be on a mountain bike. I'll introduce you to this brand new sport—which I've taken the liberty to name "all-terrain touring"—by quickly comparing two rides in Arizona.

The first was the final leg of my world ride ten years ago. It happened to be late fall when we made it to the states, and later still when all evidence of illnesses picked up in India were gone. My friend and I were on narrow tires, of course, and thus the overriding concern of hitting snow at mountain passes.

Upon reaching Phoenix we learned of the famous Apache Trail, twenty-five miles of dirt and rock winding through the Mazatzal Mountains. The sometimes hard-packed road, we were told, was extremely steep in places, and the rough terrain was worsened still by rocks fallen from hillsides. Yet this path lay like coiled ribbon astride a

50

long red gorge, cut through the millenia by the bright blue Salt River. And it ended at a dam built long ago of masonry, which looked like a castle guarding its mountain lake.

We told ourselves the bikes could take it, that it was worth the broken spokes, damaged rims and teeth-chattering rides on washboards. The more we heard the stronger our desire, but in the end we stayed with pavement, fearing breakdowns and delays.

That left us only US 60, up and over the Mogollon Rim, for fear of the first light snows which often come at that time of year. We'd talked of riding a paved portion of Coronado's Trail, one hundred miles of mountains he traversed in 1540. Again we'd heard of lovely scenery, of deep green conifer forests and crystalline lakes, of steep climbs and tough times for *any* kind of travel. But we also heard of passes nearly ten thousand feet high. Fear of snow again made us avoid it.

Ten years later I returned. Not on a touring bike, nor in late fall. I was instead on a TREK 850 ATB, and this time it was winter.

Once again Arizona was but a piece of a longer ride, the Gila Trail from San Diego to Santa Fe. I came in from across the California deserts, spent a day at Yuma to recuperate, and struck out along the Gila River. Outfitted with the Carlisle "R/T" tires mentioned earlier (26x2.10, 65psi, raised center bead), the paved miles passed quickly. I rode the rough Apache Trail, followed Coronado, even dipped far south to Tombstone for solo rides in areas where I saw few other souls. I took roads that looked like reddened scars across the backs of mountains, and trails which led to cavalry outposts and Cochise's stronghold.

The bike handled beautifully. It carried me through snow at high passes, where I reduced tire pressure by twenty pounds to increase traction. I used the same technique in desert scrub, where surfaces were soft, and tracked the creatures which had sped across at night. Their footprints were followed easily, as my position in the saddle, low gearing and great maneuverability took me along at almost a walker's pace. Yet unlike those on foot, all my supplies were carried comfortably. I had ridden more than a hundred miles in a single day on pavement, yet now on that same bike crept quietly through scrub.

On good dirt roads I pumped the tires up again and had the roller-coaster fun of flying through the hills and turns. Twice I made base camp in the wild, stored my gear, and with only one pannier and water rode into the hills. Hiding my bike in a ravine, I'd climb upon the rocks till twilight, enjoy the desert stillness through the night, and towns and motel rooms next day.

I'd never had a trip like this, where I could ride wherever I wished *and* in any season. The versatility is purchased at the cost of slower travel, and of a heavier bike. But greater time for observation makes the first drawback acceptable, and low gears handle the weight.

Just as there are times when I use narrow tire bikes for city travel, there are also times when I'd prefer to travel fast. If the region is devoid of backwoods roads, or if I'm heading coast-to-coast, I'll choose my touring bike. But for those shorter rides, of single states or two-week trips, or even longer jaunts when you're not pressed for time, give it a try. All-terrain touring is one compromise you'll *want* to live with.

Preparing for the Tour

My earlier comments in chapters dealing with preparations for trail and city riding are appropriate here, for one encounters similar conditions on the road. Your geographic region and season of travel will have an effect upon the equipment you choose, but some things—racks, panniers, gearing—are basic to all tours. And it is to these considerations that we'll now turn.

Gearing: Those who have toured before know of the infinite variables which have their effect upon performance—wind, hunger, thirst, amount of sleep the night before, sunburn, one's psychological state, touring weight—these and many more considerations determine how you'll handle hills and head winds on a given day. No one can merely read a map to know what gearing will be best, and no one who has toured a while will try. I've been dismayed in bike shops through the years when I've heard a salesman guarantee a customer he'll never "need" a wider range. They speak of "spin" and "overlapping gears," and take the engineer's approach to the humanities of travel.

I've taken the same hills on separate tours in widely different gears. There are Missouri Ozark ridges I've been pulling all my life; they don't change, but I seem to each time and shift to fit the difference. The wiser touring cyclist, I believe, will shun advice to shave two ounces by foregoing larger chainrings, or save on grams by concentrating on close-spaced freewheel cogs. Widen that range as I suggested earlier in Chapter Four, and carry the assurance both of speed *and* ease when you can use it. A low-end gear in the mid-20s will let you crank up walls, and a high-end of almost 100 will let you fly when it's all tail winds and downhill.

Fenders: A must in winter. They weren't available when I rode the Gila Trail; I pulled into a trading post on a reservation in New Mexico looking like I made my living racing motorcycles in dirt. (comments in Chapter Four)

Mirror: Always ride with one, and use it. (comments in Chapter Four)

Tent: Experience—that great but ruthless teacher—proved to me one cold November that one must choose his tent most carefully when cycling in the West. We were sixty miles from any town, camped on slickrock at the lip of a thousand foot gorge. Far below lay the gray, roiling waters of the Colorado River, to which we would descend at dawn. Two days of tremendous labor had been necessary to put us at that point, but packing all our gear down to the water's edge—through a notch cut in the rock by pioneers a century before—promised to be harder still. We needed rest.

Over the years I've used a dozen tents, and had trouble only once in keeping one erected. The problem then was loose sand in the Middle East, when pegs pulled free during the night. But this time, in the high desert in near winter, with storm clouds coming overhead and north winds turning sharp and cold, it was impossible even to make them stand for a moment. The slickrock was hard and smooth and unaccepting; we next tied off our lines to shadscale brush, our panniers, even the top tubes of our bikes. But none of these would hold in the winds that howled that evening.

The rain began two hours after dark, great sheets of it which pummeled us in successive broadsides. We lay there cold and shivering, our tents wrapped around us like huge envelopes. Wet in an instant, we were soaked in the first half hour of an all-night rain.

Such was my conversion to self-supporting tents. I've used one now across eight states, and found it invaluable. Although it weighs more than I prefer (4 lbs. 14 oz.)—especially for solo rides—its ease of assembly, rigid structure, large interior space, overall design and *reliability* make the tent worth every ounce. Waterproof when wearing its heavy-duty fly, it nevertheless prohibits condensation with a huge double-arched screened ceiling. (This screened area also makes warm weather camping pleasant, as it allows far greater air flow than most tents.) And the fly encloses enough *extra* room to keep my panniers dry. (Moss "Starlet"—two man—address in Appendix).

For that tour where weight is a greater concern than comfort, I pack the "Ultra Bivy" by Kangaroo. It's waterproof, breathable, and warm; a Texolite radiant barrier adds up to 25° F to the temperature inside. In summer that means one can travel without a sleeping bag in some areas, in winter it's like adding a comforter.

Sleeping bag: I've told the story many times. I took a sleeping bag made of down on my world ride, dropped feathers across four continents, and nearly froze in the Rockies. Down can't be washed along the trail, loses at least three-quarters of its warmth when wet, and costs a bundle. It is lightweight, and compresses better than all other fabrics. But that's of little consolation when you're wet and cold.

For a decade now I've gone with man-made products, testing FiberFill, Hollofil and, for this last year the newest entry—Quallofil. Along the Gila Trail, for Sherman's March in Georgia and on Midwest rides I've packed the Coleman "Peak 1" bag. Rated at -5°F, it takes rough treatment well. Zipper baffles prevent the escape of heat, zipper guards make zipping very easy—even in the dark. The Quallofil insulation is ninety to ninety-five per cent as compactable as down, retains ninety-five per cent of its warmth when wet, and is machine washable. But one complaint: the oxford stuffsack it comes in isn't waterproof. Kangaroo, however, makes a great "Mountain Stuff Sack" for just such times. (Coleman is the newest entry into the biking realm. They're now producing "ultralight" bags, Gore-tex shells and rainsuits. Address in Appendix)

Ground pad: No matter how good your nylon roof or the Quallofil below you, you've got to have a ground pad in cold weather. I ride with a three-quarter length Ensolite closed cell pad, one-quarter inch thick. Closed cell pads are impervious to water, great for insulation, lightweight and relatively inexpensive. But they don't provide a Serta Perfect sleep. If you're into comfort you'll have to swallow extra cost and ounces; try the self-inflating "Therm-a-Rest."

Panniers: I've already suggested the best way to buy bags: first request a catalogue from all the companies listed in the Appendix, then view the ones available at cycle shops. (Because Needle Works packs are not available in bike shops, the company offers a thirty day money-back guarantee.) Next, look through recent bicycle magazines for new manufacturers offering panniers, and talk with anyone you know who tours. As individual riders have their own opinions of "best" bike, "necessary" gear range and "the" equipment list, so it is also impossible to say one set of bags is best for all.

Well, not impossible. A veritable cornucopia of articles pours forth each year in magazines describing "impartial" tests of panniers applied by "objective" examiners reported by writers who are "above the fray." And each year the bike bag companies worry anew, fearing that some publisher will call a competitor's "best."

It's a shame. Caught between high priced space age fabrics and tight-fisted recession age consumers, pannier manufacturers can ill afford bad press. Like "expert" analysts who differ radically in opinions depending upon which school of psychology they belong to, the pros in cycling tend to judge panniers according to what's most important to them. Lately, some seem mesmerized with stability, probably because it's quantifiable. For others it's the ease of removal, number of exterior pockets, overall volume, fabric used, durability of construction, color or cost. The problem is that while one pannier might indeed be most stable, this factor is of minor importance to the person who carries little weight, wants the fastest possible removal/reattachment time, and is working within a very tight budget. Beauty—and the "best" pannier—is in the eyes of the beholder.

I won't therefore suggest that you "should" buy one bag over another. Instead, in the Appendix I'll quickly describe the panniers I've tested on the road, list what I did and didn't like, and hope that you proceed thoughtfully, logically, and independently from there. (Prices fluctuate so often that I've learned to avoid listing them. Pannier styles and mounting systems can also change over time; be sure to write for the catalogue of current models.)

And a final note of guidance in that pursuit. Think hard about how you intend to use your bags. If it's strictly touring which you have in mind then ease in mounting and removal will be less important than stability—bags seldom come off during tours. But if they're also to serve as your commuting bags then easy mounting is more important. And to make decisions even harder, I've learned through switching bags with fellow riders while on tour that cyclists often don't agree on what is and is not "easy mounting."

So pore over the catalogues, don't be afraid to mix systems, and give the choice some time. After all, this isn't a car you're buying, to be sold or junked in a few years. *These* bags will last a lifetime.

Footwear: I'm often asked about footwear. For cool to hot weather riding I use the Nike "Lava Dome," a lugged below-the-ankle hiking shoe which provides great support and is light in weight. In cold weather I've been pleased with the performance of the incredibly lightweight yet rigid Nike "Approach" hiking boot. This model is high enough (just over the ankle) to retard water entry, yet still sufficiently low to allow unimpeded pedalling. Gore-tex/leather uppers and a wide, full tongue also serve to keep the feet dry. I recommend that you look for similar features as you shop for footwear. I purchased my "Lava Dome" hiking shoes at the beginning of '84, and was in them for some eight to ten thousand miles of riding in that year. And though they were comfortable from the start I liked them even more when Spenco shoe inserts were added.

Touring Checklist

Tools:
crescent wrench (1)
screwdriver (1)
needle-nose pliers (1)
channel locks (1)
tire levers (2)
allen wrenches
cone wrenches (2)
chain rivet tool (1)
spoke wrench (1)
freewheel tool (1)
cotterless crank removal tool (1)
Swiss Army knife (1)
pocket vise (1)

Shelter and Bedding:
tent (1)
sleeping bag (1)
ground pad (1)

Medical Supplies:
sunshade (1 bottle)
aspirin (20)
snakebite kit (1)
Desitin (1 tube)
hydrogen peroxide (1 bottle)
Band-aids (10)
butterfly closure bandages (6)
combat bandage (1)
gauze compress pads (4-8)
gauze (1 roll)
ace bandage (2)
petroleum jelly (1 tube)
Benadryl (1 bottle)
insect repellent (1 bottle)
water purification tablets (1 bottle)
moleskin/2nd skin

Clothing:
T-shirts (3)
long-sleeved shirt (1)
riding shorts (2)
belt (1)
undershorts (3)
long pants (1)
gym shorts (1)
insulated underwear (1 pair)
Protogs (1 pair leggings)
socks (3 pairs)
riding shoes (1 pair)
camp moccasins (1 pair)
bandanas (2)
riding gloves (1 pair)
baseball cap (1)

Foul and Cold Weather Gear:
boots (1 pair)
neck gaiter (1)
wool cap (1)
jacket (1)
gloves (1 pair)
poncho (1)
rain chaps (1 pair)
rain suit (1)
rain cap (1)
rain boots (1)
goggles (1)
down or fiberfill jacket (1)

Personal:
towel (1)
washcloth (1)
soap (1)
soapdish (1)
toothbrush (1)
toothbrush case (1)
tooth powder (1 bottle)
comb (1)
toilet paper (20 sheets)
deodorant (1)
shampoo (1 bottle)
waterless hand cleaner (1 tube)
nail brush (1)
fingernail clipper (1)

Bike Parts:
brake cables (2)
gear cables (2)
brake pads (2)
ball bearings
bearing grease (1 tube)
oil (1 bottle)
chain links (5)
tube (1)
tire (1)
shock cords (2)
spokes (6)
riding flag (1)
fenders
air pump (1)
air gauge (1)
luggage racks (2)
water bottles
reflectors
lock and cable (1)
rear view mirror (1)
tube repair kit (1)

Miscellaneous:
pocket knife (1)
sheath knife (1)
sunglasses/case (1)
flashlight/batteries (1)
camera/film (1)
rope (15')
ripstop repair tape (6")
matches (1 box)
notebook (1)
book (1)
pen (1)
safety pins (10)
sewing kit (1)
cup (1)
utensil set (1)
can opener (1)
panniers (1 set)
pannier rain covers (1 set)
pants clips (2)
map (1)
compass (1)
candle lantern (1)
candles (2)

PART TWO

CHAPTER SIX

MECHANICS

A lot of people dread the thought of working on their bikes. They think of it as they do a trip to the dentist, as unpleasant but sometimes necessary. They picture themselves with grease-blackened hands, unhappy, in the middle of a circle of tools and pieces of a disassembled bike, worried that they're doing something wrong.

Yet there's little reason for such fears. Bicycles are beautifully simple creatures. Most troubles can be avoided by timely maintenance, by learning to listen to the sounds a bike makes, and by distinguishing between the feel of a sick and a well-tuned mount. Such sensitivity comes with time, but I've found it comes much faster to those who understand how their bikes are put together.

ATBs are even easier to care for than touring bikes, for two reasons. First, their amazing durability means fewer repairs. I have many thousands of touring, trail and commuting miles on mine, and have never had to replace a spoke, flatten a blip, or even true a wheel. I've had only one flat in all that time. And sealed pedals, hubs and bottom brackets greatly extend the intervals between bearing work.

A second reason for such easy care is the nature of the bike's design. Most components are removed with a large, easily handled 6mm allen (or hex) wrench; axle nuts are big and obvious in purpose, and little else on the bike is so delicate that it will break if tackled somewhat incorrectly. These are important features on bikes which are often taken apart to clean away the mud of trail riding.

With that aspect of ATBs in mind, of sloppy times and parts jarred loose or damaged in a fall, detailed drawings of components are very helpful. SunTour, Shimano, Specialized, and other manufacturers or their dealers will provide "exploded diagrams" and other graphic aids that will serve as reassuring guides to the neophyte mechanic. Addresses are provided in an Appendix. And TREK Bicycle Corporation has provided the drawings of various assemblies which will greatly assist you in repairs and maintenance—no matter the brand of your bike or components.

THE FRAME

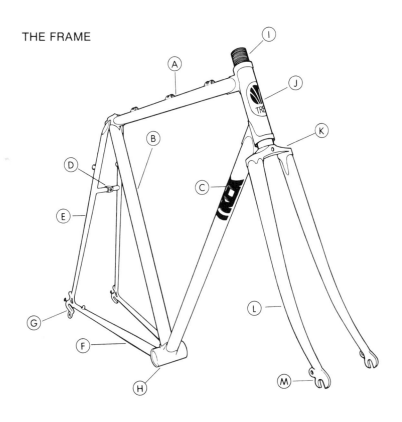

Ⓐ	Top tube	Ⓗ	Bottom bracket
Ⓑ	Seat tube	Ⓘ	Steerer tube
Ⓒ	Down tube	Ⓙ	Head tube
Ⓓ	Brake bridge	Ⓚ	Fork crown
Ⓔ	Seatstay	Ⓛ	Fork blade
Ⓕ	Chainstay	Ⓜ	Fork tip
Ⓖ	Dropout		

THE DRIVETRAIN

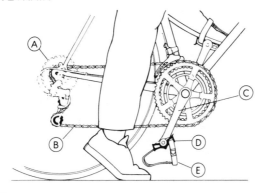

Ⓐ Freewheel		Ⓓ Pedal	
Ⓑ Chain		Ⓔ Toeclip assembly	
Ⓒ Crankset			

Part Two begins with a description of the tools I've found most useful for working on my bike at home; one can get by with less, many cyclists use far more. As with equipment lists, "the" proper tool depends as much on the mechanic as on the apparatus being fixed. I've known people who in the first excited flush of their return to biking drop a lot of money on all kinds of gear and tools, without easing into the discovery of what they might later find they'd *prefer* to own. In short, my suggestion is that you proceed through all your purchases in biking just as you ride through city streets—cautiously, with eyes wide open and hands always near the brakes.

After the suggested tool list you'll find the instructions, drawings and explanations designed to step you through your hours spent with a wrench in hand. I've supplied the information, but if you fail to match it with patience you'll have a disagreeable and probably unproductive time. Don't rush into things. In teaching cycle mechanics over the years I've often watched people move directly into the disassembly of whichever component they thought was causing problems. Parts were set haphazardly on the floor or nearby workbench, out of sequence, uninspected, unknown in purpose or relationship to their fellows—and therefore likely to be lost. Study your bike *before* you begin working on it, and then proceed thoughtfully.

CHAPTER SEVEN

TOOLS

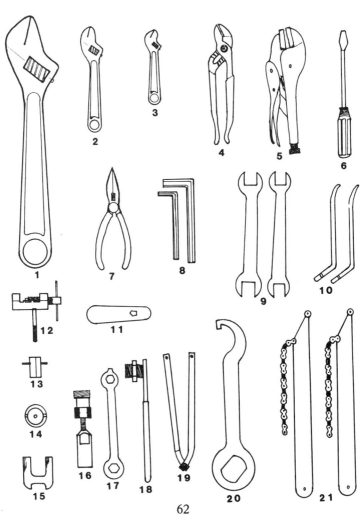

1. *Crescent wrench - 15"*: Don't buy one if you already own a good vise or large pipe wrench; one of the three is necessary to pull your crank and freewheel.

2. *Crescent wrench - 6"*: Perhaps the tool used most often on touring bikes, the 6" crescent is eclipsed by allen wrenches on an ATB. However, one is still necessary for wheel axle nuts, and on some models for much more. Buy a quality crescent; the slide mechanism on a cheap one will in time refuse to stay cinched tightly against a nut. It will round off corners and bring on expletives and another trip to the store. Don't use it for pulling cranks or freewheels unless you're on the road and far away from anyone who might have something larger; you can damage the slide and jaws of the tool in this way.

3. *Crescent wrench - 4"*: You won't need this size if you buy a set of metric open or box end wrenches. But if that luxury is postponed you'll find the 4" is a nice tool for brake work; considerably smaller in size than its 6" brother, it fits more easily in tight places and allows a more sensitive gauging of the torque applied to smaller nuts. Again, don't skimp when buying tools unless you like repeat purchases and poor performances.

4. *Channel locks - 7"*: A good road tool for headsets which need tightening, and anything else which may require wide jaws and a strong grip. Before the SunTour "Pocket Vise" came about I used to use the channel locks, a bungie wound around the handles and profanity to back off freewheels while on tour.

5. *Vise grips:* In recent years some companies have begun to offer very small vise grips, which are excellent when doing fine work which requires both hands free. But a larger vise grip is needed to remove blips from rim walls—especially with the wide rims of mountain bikes. Buy accordingly.

6. *Regular blade screwdriver:* As described in Chapter Three, I carry a short handled, long shanked one of 6" overall length, with a flat blade tip only 3/16" wide. This size allows for very fine adjustments of derailleur set screws.

7. *Needle-nose pliers:* Choose a small pair with side-cutters (for trimming brake and gear cables), and notice when you're buying how well the tips come together.

8. *Allen wrenches:* Check every allen head on your bike to be sure you have the right sizes, for almost nothing else will work if the bolt is

tight, and everything used in a pinch (a smaller hex held at an angle, a screwdriver . . .) will in time ruin the head.

9. *Cone wrenches:* As with allens, almost nothing else will do the job. I pack along the thin, lightweight alloy kind; one with tips of 13 and 14mm, the second of 15 and 16mm. Be careful if you buy these from a catalogue, for some are "shop models" made of steel and very heavy.

10. *Tire levers:* I carry two, and have never seen anyone require the third one which often comes with the set. Be sure the tips are round and smooth before you insert them.

11. *Swiss Army knife:* Heavy and expensive, these beautifully built tools are sometimes very useful on the road. I carry one with the features I need most as a cyclist: a metal file blade to file off protruding spoke heads, a phillips screwdriver, a large flat tip screwdriver blade, tiny forceps for splinters, and a leather punch. (The fishhook disgorger is also a 3″ rule—excellent for measuring my road mileage on days of rough head winds.)

12. *Chain rivet tool:* You'll need this for removing a chain, adding links, and freeing frozen links. Ask your bike shop salesman or check the spec chart on your bike for the brand and size of your chain, and be sure you know the rivet tool you're buying will fit. (Mail-order catalogues usually specify which chains their tools will fit, as will the instruction sheet accompanying the tool.)

13. *Spoke nipple wrench:* I prefer the "T" type to the round multi-size style, for I seem to get a sharper feel of the spoke tension. Just be sure it's large enough to fit the nipples on your all-terrain.

14. *Freewheel tool:* There are many kinds, and some companies have more than one configuration freewheel tool for the models of freewheels they manufacture. Over the last two years the majority of mountain bikes have come equipped with SunTour freewheels, but make sure which kind you have before you buy the matching tool.

15. *Pocket vise:* A two-ounce answer to broken spokes on the freewheel side when you're on the road. (SunTour was the first company out with one, but others are now available under a generic label.)

16. *Cotterless crank removal tool:* A different kind is made for every brand of crank.

17. *Universal cotterless crank wrench:* You'll only need this if you work on many kinds of cranks, and even then it's so large and heavy that

you'll never pack it on the road. The wrench removes the crankarm fixing bolts, that wonderful advance of technology beyond the formerly ubiquitous cotter pins.

18. *Universal cotterless crankarm puller:* A tool for home use only, and then only if you work on several different model cranks. As the name implies the tool removes the crankarm.

19. *Universal adjustable cup tool:* For home use only. On the road I use the leather punch of my Swiss Army knife, a screwdriver blade or the needle-nose tip to adjust the bottom bracket bearing pressure.

20. *Lock ring/fixed cup bottom bracket tool:* Too heavy for the road, this is a wise purchase to save the fittings on the adjustable crank bearing cup. It is also almost the only thing which will remove the fixed cup side, and even then not easily.

21. *Freewheel sprocket tools:* Home use only. You'll need only one if you have access to a large vise, two if you don't. And you won't need any if you think you'll never want to change the sprockets. (Smaller sprockets of course wear more quickly; many people toss entire freewheels when four cogwheels are still good, or when just the body—the center core with all the tiny bearings—needs to be junked.)

22. *Sealed bearing tools* (not pictured): Most mountain bikes have "sealed" bearings in one or more areas—pedals, headset, hubs, bottom bracket. Many of these seals can be removed easily with one or more of the tools above, but some (like Eclipse hubs) are more conveniently removed with specific tools made for this purpose. Your dealer will point out these seals to you and will either have the appropriate tool for sale or can order it. Don't be afraid to ask that he show you how to use it, but be prepared to return to the shop at some time of *his* convenience for the instruction. (If your schedule allows it try to hit bike shops at times other than Friday afternoons and Saturdays; it seems everyone on those two days requests "immediate" help for weekend riding.)

For easier repairs and tune-ups at home, you might consider a bike stand. There are of course shop models for the well-heeled sophisticate, and mid-range stands which still hold both wheels completely off the ground. But a very useful and yet inexpensive stand is of the style used in shops to display the bikes for sale; the rear wheel alone is held above the floor. (The rear wheel must be free to rotate for adjustments to derailleurs.)

Wheel truing stands also make one's job much easier, though I've always done this work by simply flipping the bike on its back. Crude perhaps and a pain due to cables, thumb shifters and bells, it nevertheless is the manner required on the road. But if you have the room in a garage or basement I suggest an inexpensive stand, even though your mountain bike wheel may never require it.

The last item I keep at home is a floor pump with built-in gauge. The larger ATB tires require less pressure than their thinner cousins, but there's still a larger area to fill. (And I *hate* using hand pumps, especially with a hand-held gauge which lets out much of that hard-earned air.)

CHAPTER EIGHT

HANDLEBARS, STEM, HEADSET

Imagine the consequences if your bars pull free in the middle of a bunny hop or if your wheel remains pointing straight ahead as you turn the bars to escape an oncoming bus. Well, don't concentrate too long on those unpleasant thoughts, for they'll probably never take place even if you abuse your bike mechanically. But you can make *sure* it will never happen by understanding the function and design of these components, and thereby knowing if they begin to loosen up.

HEADSET

(A) Lock nut
(B) Lock washer
(C) Adjusting cup/cone
(D) Bearings
(E) Top head race
(F) Bottom head race
(G) Crown race

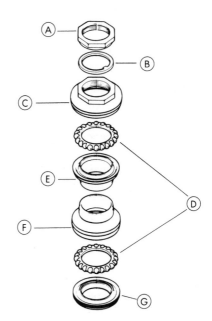

67

We all know the function of the handlebars—you steer with them. They're the straight-line driver's wheel, a three foot bit in the bike's teeth, and are piled high with cushion grips, thumb shifters, brake handles, fingerbells, lights, camera, and far more action than you think. And that's because of its attachment (via the stem) to the headset—that unappreciated unit which holds your bars and front wheel on the bike.

The bars, stem and headset on a mountain bike are put under enormous strain from the off-road, off-curb riding style. In Chapter Two I spoke of the preferable "triangulated" alloy stem, preferred due to light weight and the tremendous strength of the design. But this attachment system also allows an air traveler to ship his bike most easily, without touching his headset at all. Strength *and* convenience— just like the bike itself.

Difficulties and desired adjustments to the bars and headset are discussed in the following categories:

1. handlebar removal for air travel
2. bar height adjustment
3. loose bars—movement side to side
4. tight bars—difficult to turn side to side
5. handgrips

1. **Handlebar removal for air travel:**
Some airlines do not require passengers to box their bikes. But they do demand that bars be turned and pedals removed. On a touring bike this means a loosening of the headset, but with most mountain bikes a single allen wrench and four bolts are all that's involved. Merely back out the bolts, remove the metal clasps which the bolts hold in position, and lift off the bar. You may have to disengage the front brake cable before you can lift the bars. If so, merely reach down to the "wire end fixture"—see Shimano "Center Wire Assembly" drawing on next page—free it from the "hook link," and lift the brake cable from the "cable carrier." To avoid loss, immediately replace the metal clasps and bolts, and tighten sufficiently so that they won't back out from vibration. Then turn the handlebar—still with all gear and brake cables attached—until it's parallel with and alongside the top tube. At this point either bungie it in place, or tape it securely. The remaining stem provides enough of a grip for steering the bike through the airport.

Most bull moose bars have a slight bend near either end, and the exact angle of those ends can be changed—pointed up or down—by loosening the four bolts and two metal clasps mentioned above, and rotating the handlebars.

CENTER WIRE ASSEMBLY

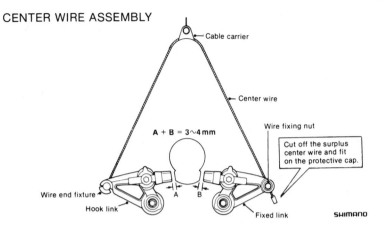

Cable carrier

Center wire

Wire fixing nut

A + B = 3~4mm

Cut off the surplus center wire and fit on the protective cap.

Wire end fixture

Hook link

A B

Fixed link

SHIMANO

2. Bar height adjustment:

Begin this task with the same approach you should take to all mechanical chores—a quick study of what will be involved, followed by a plan of attack. X-ray vision would help. But if you lack that talent refer to the diagram, and notice the allen head (usually 6mm) expander bolt. At the other end of this bolt—inside the head tube—is either an angled expander nut or a wedge nut. (Some mechanics call the former an "exterior" wedge, the latter an "interior" wedge.) When the expander bolt is tightened the angled nut presses against the head tube wall; the wedge nut type works by drawing the nut up inside the stem, forcing the stem walls out against the head tube.

STEM

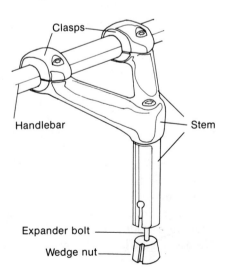

Clasps

Handlebar

Stem

Expander bolt

Wedge nut

Now that you know what goes on inside the head tube during this adjustment, look outside. The front brake cable—depending on your model bike—runs through the stem. Raise it to tighten the brakes. Lower the stem and brake cable tension is lessened.

To adjust bar height, disengage the front brake cable by pushing the "hook link" (see "Center Wire Assembly" drawing) toward the rim, and slipping the "wire end fixture" free. This allows you to remove the "cable carrier" from the center wire, thus severing the physical link between the handlebar front brake lever and the lower attachment end of the brake cable.

(That sounds extremely confusing, but only if you read it through quickly without referring to the drawings. Identify every part noted in the instructions; the procedure will then be seen as very simple.)

Next, loosen the expander bolt until you can raise or lower the handlebars. (Don't be concerned if the wedge nut comes off the expander bolt, for it can't fall far. Just turn the bike upside down and the nut will come free.) If you have loosened the bolt completely and are still unable to move the bars it is because the angle or wedge nut is frozen inside the head tube. Re-thread the expander bolt a couple of turns, then rap it with a mallet or anything similar. (Those people concerned with such things might wish to protect their expander bolt heads from scratches by covering them with a cloth or piece of wood if a metal hammer is to be used. But if you're of this type I pity you when you see what rough trail riding can do to a paint job.)

Position the bars at the desired height (being *sure* to leave a full two inches of stem below the top of the headset) and tighten the expander bolt. Then re-engage the brake cable, adjusting it appropriately. (See "Brakes" below.)

3. Loose bars—movement side to side:

You say your front wheel points straight down the road when your handlebars are looking at the curb? Easy. Road vibration or poor original installation has jarred loose the angle or wedge nut. Realign the bars and wheels and tighten the expander bolt.

4. Tight bars—difficult to turn side to side:

Don't blame the bars. This is the headset's fault. The headset secures the fork to the frame, but must also allow for free turning of the fork to either side. The diagram of the headset and fork will show how this dual purpose is made possible: the top tube of the fork is threaded, and held in place in the head tube by the top threaded race (adjusting cup). This race, and the fork crown race, are positioned with the top and bottom bearings to allow for rotation.

Two things can cause problems with side to side movement—the bearings might require lubrication, or, as is usually the case, the adjusting cup is simply screwed down too tight. In the first instance, loosen the large lock nut at the top of the headset (using the large crescent if home, the channel locks on the road). Next, loosen the adjusting cup, but only slightly—until you can see the bearings inside—but stop before they can leap out and hide on the floor. Squirt cycle oil into the mass of bearings, very carefully allow the fork to slip down a fraction of an inch to expose the bottom bearings, and oil there. This done, tighten the adjusting cup, then the lock nut on top, until there is no upward or downward movement within the headset, but free movement of the fork and bars from side to side. (Your top and bottom bearings may be set inside a small retainer. If so, you stand a small chance of losing them; apply oil as indicated. A good bearing grease, like Philwood, is actually preferable to oil. But its application in this instance is more difficult for quick road maintenance.)

If you drop bearings out of the headset, and do not know if they came from the top or bottom race, you'll have to take all the bearings out of both, divide them in half and replace them. (There should be a slight gap present—less than a bearing's width—when the proper number of bearings are in a race.) If you come up with an odd number of bearings, even after searching everywhere, be sure to replace it with exactly the same size ball. Your bike shop will have them. (Headset bearings are usually 5/32".)

The second movement problem, that of adjustment alone, is much more simple. Back off the lock nut, turn the adjusting cup until free movement side to side is reached without upward or downward movement of the fork through the headset, and re-tighten. As with many components on your bike you'll notice that adjusting cups tighten against the bearings slightly when lock nuts are secured. Try leaving the adjusting cup slightly more loose than you wish it to be, knowing it will gain an eighth of a turn or so when the lock nut is tightened.

Bearings in headsets and pedals usually last for years if lubricated occasionally and not abused by riding with them misadjusted. Wheel and crank bearings, on the other hand, require more attention. But when does a ball bearing need to be replaced? Every time you service wheels and bottom brackets check to see that all bearings are round and smooth on the surface. Sand and the usual road grime will tend to "pit" bearings, and after a while will flake off a piece of the surface. If these bearings remain in your bike they will wear upon axles and races until those too require replacement. Bearings are extremely inexpensive compared to those parts. So don't forget the axiom about an ounce of prevention.

5. Handgrips:

After many months of daily commuting and trail riding, and six weeks into a tour, the great spongy feeling of my handgrips gave out. These are easily replaced: pull off the plastic bar end caps (I used my channel locks), peel off the grips, and slide new ones into place. This last step is made easier by sprinkling the metal bar grip area with talc, dust or flour. Replace the bar end cap.

I couldn't find replacement grips on tour, and so bought a small sheet of leather, cut it into strips, and wrapped both grips. A curved needle and large gauge waxed thread was then used to secure it. This cushioned my hands from the metal bar, but somewhat reduced my grip (except when the leather was wet with perspiration).

I usually avoid riding gloves, but have tested a Spenco pair recently and found them well-made and most comfortable. The Spenco "Palm Pads," held in place by wrist and finger loops, are especially convenient for hot desert travel. Omission of the cycling gloves' leather loops and cloth netting makes for a cooler ride. I've also used a palm pad beneath a regular cold weather glove on tour, to cushion an injured hand.

CHAPTER NINE

SADDLES AND SEATPOSTS

Many mountain bikes come equipped with single allen-head bolt adjustable Laprade seatposts ("A" micro adjust style in drawing), which make three of the suggested adjustments below extremely easy. The fourth—height—is made simple by the quick-release seatpost feature, replacing the touring bike "binder bolt." Most riders apparently think only of height in reference to saddle position, and so forego the better ride and feel available through seatpost and saddle design. Those adjustments for correct fit are:

1. height
2. tilt
3. forward/backward position
4. side to side position

SADDLE AND SEATPOST

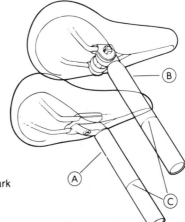

Ⓐ Micro adjust
Ⓑ Integral seatpost
Ⓒ Minimum insertion mark

1. **Height:**

Except for trail and snow riding, I position my mountain bike saddle exactly as on my touring bike—at a height which allows for full leg extension during pedal rotation (with only the ball of my foot on the pedal). This avoids the cramping of leg muscles, and also makes possible the very efficient pedalling technique of "ankling."

To attain this efficiency, begin by adjusting your saddle height so that when the pedal is at the end of its down-stroke (6 o'clock) it is too low for your instep or heel to reach it—just the ball of your foot should be on the pedal. At the top of the up-stroke (12 o'clock), the heel should be *below* the pedal; the foot is actually pointing up slightly at this time. Now, on the beginning down-stroke not only will the thigh and calf muscles be used for propulsion, but those in the foot arch will assist by adding the mechanical fulcrum action. The result is the greatest possible application of muscle to the task. Efficiency is aided further by mountain bike pedal clips (some people even use clips *and* straps on ATBs), for the foot then assists the opposite pedal on its up-stroke.

Attain this desired saddle height by simply flipping the quick-release seatpost lever and raising or lowering the post. *Caution:* Leave a full two inches of post in the seat tube. Also, be sure that the quick-release lever is completely re-engaged before riding.

2. `Tilt:`

Only during the last decade have saddle makers begun to take into account the differences of male and female anatomy, and to offer a wide range of padded thicknesses. Spenco has more recently offered a "Bio-Soft Polymer" saddle cover, which feels like one has slipped on a pair of riding shorts made of live eels. (The touring cyclist will decry the cover's weight, but only after he is over those terrible first days of being saddle sore; if you haven't lost this soreness in training rides before the trip you can always begin with the cover and then, when you toughen up, send it home.) There are also saddles offered now which completely destroy the aesthetic appeal of bikes, by replacing the graceful, sloping curve of leather with a sling or double-cup affair.

But with all these appeals to comfort, many riders are unaware that they can alter the tilt of their present saddles to increase riding ease. Look at the "Saddle and Seatpost" drawing. You can see that each saddle underside has two long metal bars which run nearly the length of the seat, and which are wider toward the rear, narrower toward the front or nose of the saddle. Attached to these bars on "B" is a double clamp with a hole in the center for the seatpost, and a single metal bar threaded on both ends. This bar runs through the two clamps and has a nut on either end. Tighten the nut and the clamps tighten upon the long metal bars beneath the seat, while also narrowing the center hole and thereby securing the saddle to the seatpost.

The sides of these double clamps have grooves or serrated edges to keep the saddle position from changing once the nuts are tightened against them. Alter your saddle tilt while it is mounted on the seatpost by grabbing one clamp nut with a wrench (I prefer vise grips) and holding it fast. With a second wrench (6" crescent, my choice) loosen the second clamp nut until it moves freely; then, apply force to the saddle rear or nose to move it into place. Finally, tighten the clamp nut securely.

If your mountain bike comes with a "micro adjust" seatpost (or if you upgrade to one) you own an infinitely superior design. You'll appreciate it if you've ever had the double clamp model completely apart—seven independent pieces of nuts, clamps and threaded bar trying their best not to work in unison. Compare this to a single 6mm allen wrench adjustment point: merely loosen, apply pressure to the saddle heel or nose to obtain desired tilt, and tighten.

A third style saddle clamp (thankfully far less common than the micro-adjust) has two bolts pointing downward from beneath the saddle, therefore making it quite difficult to reach the bolt head with a regular wrench. Special wrenches are available for this purpose, which are bent like a flattened "S". Choose the micro-adjust model if you can.

3. Forward/backward position:

This is a far more important adjustment than tilt, yet is also seldom considered. The saddle position forward and backward determines the rider's reach to the handlebars, and thereby his back posture, and arm and shoulder bearing. Experiment with this fitting until you find the best position, given your particular bar and saddle height.

To slide the saddle forward or backward merely loosen the clamp nuts or allen bolt as in "2" above, position the saddle where you wish, and tighten the nuts or allen bolt once more.

4. Side to side movement:

The nose of the saddle should point directly forward over the bicycle top tube, but sometimes will become cocked to one side or the other. To straighten this you should, as in "1" above, loosen the seatpost quick-release, position the saddle correctly, and tighten.

CHAPTER TEN

DERAILLEURS

This component group is your bike's transmission system—a real workhorse which allows you access to a wide range of gear ratios. *Derailler* in French means "to take from the rails." In cycling it refers to the movement of one's chain from one cogwheel or sprocket to another. The system is composed of thumb shifters, gear cables, and front and rear derailleurs.

FRONT DERAILLEUR

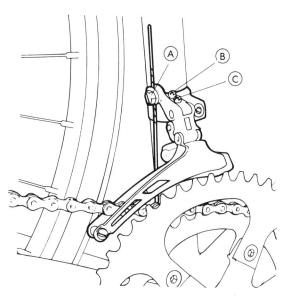

Ⓐ Cable clamp bolt   Ⓒ High gear adjusting screw
Ⓑ Low gear adjusting screw

REAR DERAILLEUR

REAR DERAILLEUR
ALIGNMENT

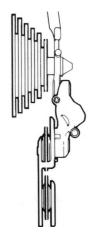

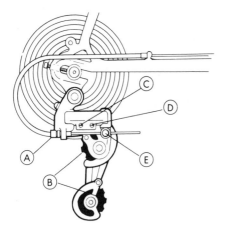

Ⓐ Adjusting barrel
Ⓑ Derailleur pulleys
Ⓒ Low gear adjusting screw
Ⓓ High gear adjusting screw
Ⓔ Cable clamp bolt

When adjusting rear derailleur, pulleys should be on the same plane as the smallest freewheel sprocket.

I've had people tell me they never shift gears, that it's too complicated, or that they don't ride enough to bother with it. Follow along on your bike as you read this section and the concept and function of this system will become very easy to understand.

1. basic operation
2. cable replacement/adjustment
3. rear derailleur problems
4. front derailleur problems

1. Basic operation:

Basically, a gear cable runs from the thumb shifters, along the down tube and chain stay, through a cable adjusting barrel, to a cable clamp bolt on the changer (derailleur). When you push forward on the shifter lever you tighten the cable, which causes the derailleur to lift the chain from a smaller sprocket, and set it upon a larger one. Naturally, there are limits to how far in either direction you would wish your chain to go, and this limitation is established and maintained by "high" and "low" gear adjusting screws. The high gear screw on rear derailleurs keeps the chain from moving beyond the smallest sprocket and falling off the freewheel; the low gear screw keeps the chain from moving beyond the largest sprocket and attacking your spokes. The third screw present on some changers is an "angle" screw. Chains, like cables, stretch in time, and thereby change the angle of the derailleur and thus its performance. This angle screw allows for taking up this tiny bit of slack, by resetting the proper angle in relation to the freewheel.

Below the derailleur housing are two pulleys, or rollers. Notice that the chain rolls over one and under the second. The top pulley is the "jockey" or "guide" pulley—named for its job of jockeying the chain into place over a sprocket. The bottom one is the "tension" pulley, for it takes up the slack in the chain when the derailleur moves from a larger to a smaller sprocket. The final thing you should notice is the points of lubrication. Simply apply two drops of oil every month to all springs and moving parts, then wipe off the excess.

2. Cable replacement/adjustment:

Begin by studying the thumb shifter and drawings of the front and rear derailleur. Next, loosen the "cable fixing bolt" (or "cable clamp bolt") of whichever derailleur is affected by the broken cable, and remove the cable. (If the rear derailleur cable has broken, screw the "cable adjusting barrel" clockwise—into the derailleur body—until it stops.) Then turn to the thumb shifter, remove the lever fixing bolt and cover (carefully! or you'll have to follow the exploded drawings to make sure all parts are replaced in correct order), install a new cable and replace the cover and fixing bolt. Put the thumb lever in its most extreme rearward (toward the saddle) position.

Feed the new cable through the cable housing (I always oil or grease the cable at this point, to avoid a "frozen" cable problem if water later enters a crack in the housing), then through the cable adjusting barrel (on rear derailleurs), and on to the cable fixing bolt.

Rear derailleur adjustment: Place the chain on the smallest front chainring. Pull the cable slightly taut (not so much that the derailleur body moves) and secure it by tightening the cable fixing bolt. The rear derailleur pulleys should be in line with the smallest freewheel sprocket at this point. If they are not, turn the "high gear adjusting screw" (or "stroke adjusting screw") until that line is attained; if it cannot be reached with the adjusting screw it means you have pulled the cable too tight. Loosen the cable fixing bolt and readjust the cable tension.

Some derailleurs have a small "H" and "L" stamped in the changer body to indicate the high and low adjusting screws, but if yours does not you'll quickly determine their location by observing which one affects the derailleur when the chain is in the smallest sprocket (high gear screw) and the largest sprocket (low gear screw) of the freewheel. To make the low gear adjustment, carefully shift the chain onto the largest freewheel sprocket; if this can't be done, turn the low gear adjusting screw counterclockwise until it can. Then adjust the thumb shifter until the rear derailleur pulleys are in perfect line with the largest freewheel sprocket, and turn the low gear adjusting screw clockwise—into the changer body—until you feel resistance.

The cable will stretch over time. When this happens take up the slack with the "cable adjusting barrel." (Metal end caps often come with cables. Prevent fraying of the cable end by slipping the end cap into place, and crimping it with needle-nose pliers or channel locks.)

Front derailleur adjustment: Place the chain on the largest rear and smallest front sprockets. Then turn the low gear adjusting screw until there's a slight clearance between the chain and the inside plate of the chain "cage" or "guide." If this cannot be done it means you have pulled the cable too taut; loosen the cable anchor bolt, correct the tension, and re-tighten.

Next, place the chain on the smallest rear and largest front sprockets. Then turn the high gear adjusting screw until there is a slight clearance between the chain and the outside plate of the chain cage (chain guide).

When these adjustments to the rear and front derailleurs have been made, switch the chain through all possible gear combinations. In each gear you should be able to position the derailleurs so that the chain does not make noise and does not rub against the metal inner and outer plates.

3. **Rear derailleur problems:**
   Problem: You can't see your derailleur any longer, and performance is impaired.

Road grime and trail mud, if not often wiped away, will build to the point that your derailleur must be removed from the bike for thorough cleaning. Proceed as follows.

a) A "bracket axle assembly," equipped with a 6mm allen bolt and affixed to the frame just behind the axle or "dropout," must first be located. Clean it sufficiently to see exactly how it is mounted; locate the "stopper plate" and observe how it overlaps the rear tip of the "fork end." ("Fork end" is the end portion of the frame into which the bracket axle screws.) Some bikes have instead a flat bracket assembly which is cut away to fit around the axle, and a single bolt and lock nut affixing it to the frame. But whichever you have (most probably the former), study it carefully to insure proper replacement after cleaning.

b) Move the thumb shift lever completely rearward (toward the saddle), loosen the cable anchor bolt on the derailleur, and remove the cable. Using the 6mm allen wrench, remove the bracket axle. This will free the derailleur from the frame—unless you've ridden through wet concrete—but you still must free it from the chain.

c) Some derailleurs have the convenient feature of an open "pulley plate assembly"—more commonly referred to as the "cage." This is the unit consisting of jockey (guide) and tension pulleys and the cage sides (inner and outer plates). The "open cage" system allows the chain to be freed without taking the cage apart; a "closed cage" requires only another minute while the bolt running through the lower (tension) pulley is removed, the pulley slipped out and the chain freed. (Another option is of course to take apart or "break" the chain with a chain rivet tool, but this is even more time consuming.)

d) When the cable has been freed from the anchor bolt and adjusting barrel, the bracket axle removed, and the chain pulled from the pulley cage, the derailleur is separated from the frame. Swish it about in a pan of gasoline or kerosene, use an old toothbrush to clean the hard to reach areas, and pay particular attention to the internal springs if your changer has them exposed. (Most mountain bikes come equipped with "sealed mechanism" derailleurs, which enclose and thereby protect the internal springs.)

e) Take apart each pulley, cleaning the bushings and caps. If you have bearing pulleys (which you won't unless you've installed them yourself) remove the cone bushings, clean and inspect each bearing, then grease and reassemble. Thread the cone into the pulley by hand, and adjust its pressure against the bearings as with all such operations— free rotation but no side-play. If your pulleys are without bearings, separate the metal bushing and side plates, clean and grease, and reassemble.

f) Wipe off all solvent from the derailleur, and allow to dry completely.

g) Place a drop of oil on moving parts and visible springs (wiping off all excess), grease the threads of the bracket axle, and re-attach the derailleur to the frame. Restore the chain to the pulley cage, replace the tension pulley, thread the cable through the cable adjusting barrel to the cable anchor bolt, and follow the "cable replacement" instructions above. (You will find this difficult if you've ridden without an end cap on the cable, and impossible if the cable tip is badly frayed. Always crimp a cap in place, or solder the tip.)

Problem: The chain slips from larger to smaller freewheel sprockets.

Most often this is caused by the thumb shifter assembly—not the derailleur or evil spirits. Think of the shifter's fate in life; it is under constant tension from the gear cable, it must respond easily to the flick of a thumb, and it must remain stationary once you have located it properly (or improperly—in which case you'll hear the chatter of metal chain on metal derailleur cage) over a sprocket. No wonder a shifter on occasion begins to lose its grip.

To restore order in its world merely tighten the lever fixing bolt. On most thumb shift models this is done by flipping up the small metal bale on the bolt head, turning it clockwise to tighten the hold upon the cable (thereby preventing further chain slippage), and reseating the bale.

If the shifter is not causing the difficulty, the culprit is the misaligned derailleur. Review the alignment procedure in "cable replacement" above, and proceed.

Problem: Your chain falls off the smallest sprocket, or jumps over the largest sprocket into the spokes, or won't quite move up enough to engage the largest sprocket, or down the freewheel to stay on the smallest.

This is exasperating, but is easily corrected by *slight* adjustments of your high or low stroke adjusting screws (chain limiting adjustment screws). Put the bike on a stand, have a friend hold the rear wheel off the ground, learn levitatation, or flip the bike on its back. Adjust the proper screw, one-eighth turn at a time. Remember—larger sprockets in the rear are affected by the low gear screw, smaller sprockets by the high gear screw.

Problem: Your derailleur moves in response to your pushing forward on the shifter (tightening the cable), but will not return to its original position when the shifter is moved back again.

a) The problem could be, but probably isn't, a very dirty derailleur. The spring in the changer, if really loaded up with road grease, or frozen by rust, will hold the changer in one place no matter the shifter and cable movement. If this is so, clean and lubricate the entire derailleur, as described above.

b) Each time I've seen the problem of a derailleur which won't budge, the solution has been to lubricate the cable. I mentioned earlier, in the discussion of brake cables, that a broken cable housing will allow water inside. This can freeze in winter, or cause rust any time of the year. So repair or replace cracked cable housing, and lubricate the dry cable with oil or grease to free it from sticking.

Problem: Your chain slips—not to another sprocket, but while on the same sprocket.

While this at first appears to be caused by the derailleur, it is actually the result of a worn freewheel sprocket. The entire freewheel—or preferably just the worn sprocket itself—must be replaced. See instructions below in "Wheels."

4. Front derailleur problems:

Problem: No matter where you place your thumb shifter the noise of chain on chain cage (or guide) continues.

a) Following the adjustment instructions above in "cable replacement," attempt to end the noise while still allowing easy shifting. If you cannot, check the position of the derailleur on the seat tube: the bottom lip of the chain guide should have a clearance of 2-3mm (⅛") over the largest chainring (chainwheel). Next, look down on the chain guide to determine its alignment with the chainring; the outside plate should be perfectly parallel with the chainring. If either the height or alignment is incorrect, loosen the derailleur clamp bolt, reposition the component, and retighten.

b) Front derailleurs are tricky beasts. I've had one which refused to be silent and still shift the chain onto the largest chainring until I adjusted the high gear screw (high gear is large sprocket in front—the opposite of the rear) so that the chain actually overshot the largest sprocket— throwing off the chain completely. I remedied this problem by grabbing the front tip (toward the handlebars) of the chain guide outer plate with my needle-nose pliers, and bending it slightly toward the frame.

c) If the chain rubs only at one spot when pedalling the problem is probably your chainring. Just as a wheel must remain "true" to keep from rubbing against the brakes, a chainring must be true or it will slap against the sides of the cage at certain spots. Sometimes the chainring bolts—the bolts which hold the front sprockets together—come loose and must be tightened. If you have done this and the wobble is still present, check to see that your bottom bracket assembly has not worked loose. While I have never been troubled by an untrue chainring which couldn't be corrected by one of these methods, you might be. If you are on tour and have no other choice, remove the sprockets and attempt, while praying fervently, to straighten them out with light hammering. But if you are at home, or in a town with a good cycle shop, I suggest you have a good shop mechanic help you.

Problem: Your front derailleur refuses to budge when you adjust the thumb shift lever, or fails to return to its original position when you release the cable tension.

The problem here is caused by either a frozen cable or a mud- or dirt-caked derailleur. Following instructions in "cable replacement" and "rear derailleur problems" above, disengage the cable, clean, lubricate, and replace. Then do the same with the derailleur if the problem persists.

CHAPTER ELEVEN

WHEELS

The wheel consists of many parts: hub assembly, spokes, freewheel in the rear, rim, tape (a cloth, plastic or rubber strip covering the spoke heads, the tape sits between the inside rim walls, protecting the tube from the spokes), tube, tire liner (optional but *strongly* suggested for commuting and cactus-area pedalling), and tire. Possible problems and suggested maintenance will be discussed in the following order.

1. flats
2. broken spokes/wheel alignment
3. bearing maintenance
4. freewheel removal/cleaning
5. freewheel disassembly

1. **Flats:**

In Part One I suggested tire liners to help avoid flats, and stated that the thick tread and high profile of ATB tires will also mean far less sidewall damage and fewer punctures. But the possibility of a flat is always present, and you should therefore know what to do.

a) Assemble the necessary tools of two tire levers, a 6″ crescent, tube repair kit or extra tube, and an air pump (or nearby service station or bike shop).

b) Remove the wheel. To do so you'll have to put your bike on a stand or on its back, loosen both axle nuts, and disengage the brake cable—so as to increase the distance between the brake pads sufficiently for the tire to pass between them—by pushing the "hook link" (see "center wire assembly" drawing in Chapter Eight) toward the rim, and slipping the "wire end fixture" free. If it's the front wheel, you can simply lift the wheel out of its dropouts at this point. On the rear wheel, shift the chain into the smallest freewheel sprocket, grab the derailleur

TIRE REMOVAL

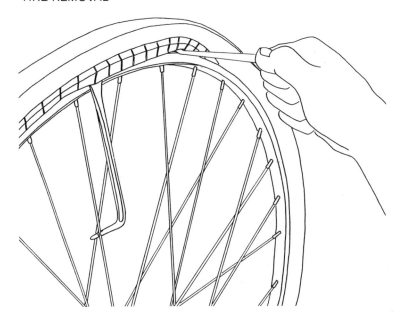

body and pull it toward the rear of the bike and lift the wheel free.

c) Remove the tire and tube from the rim. This is accomplished with the aid of your tire levers (spoons). Take the lesser angled end of one spoon and, beveled end up, work it underneath the tire bead about a half-inch. (Begin working with the first lever at a point on the wheel opposite to the valve stem. A tire's "beading" is the rubber encased metal strip which seats a "clincher" tire into the rim; "sew-ups" are the other type of tire, have no beading, and must be glued onto the rim.) Now push down on the tire lever end in your hand—that is—toward the spokes. Hook the slotted side onto a spoke to hold the tire in place—as in the drawing. (This frees both hands for the rest of the work.) Take a second lever and, once more, work the tip underneath the tire bead, about one inch from the first lever. Again, push down on your lever, to pop the bead away from its seat in the rim. If you can't do this, move your lever a half-inch closer to the first lever. Now continue to work the bead away from the rim all around the wheel, until you have one complete side of the tire off the rim. Then, using your spoon from the opposite side of the wheel, work the second bead off the rim. (You are now working the bead off the rim *away* from you in direction, as of course both beads must come off the same side to free the tire.) Taking one side of the tire off at a time is much easier than trying to force both beads off at once. (Expect a new tire to be more difficult to remove than an old one.)

d) Take the tube out of the tire, and check the outside and inside of the tire for embedded glass, thorns, etc. When you're sure that it's clean, move on to the tube. I've had only two holes in my life which leaked so little that I was forced to hold them under water to look for air bubbles. All the other times I merely pumped up the tube and listened for escaping air. (Once I heard air coming out of the center of the valve. If you look at a Schrader tube valve—the kind found on ATBs—you'll see that the inside is threaded. If the core is not screwed tightly into these threads an air leak will result. The proper tool to tighten a valve core is the valve cover tool, a tiny slotted metal cap which you should buy to replace the worthless black plastic caps present on all tubes sold. If you have a very slow leak check that your valve core is tight before you remove the wheel from the frame.)

e) When the hole is located, rough up the area with the patch kit scraper. Be sure to do a good job of it, short of putting additional holes in the tube, and be sure to roughen an area a bit larger than the size of the patch.

f) Apply the glue, again a bit more than necessary to cover the patch area. Most kits suggest waiting until the glue is dry to apply the patch. So, wait. Hurry this step and there's a good chance you'll be taking the wheel back off the bike a few miles down the road. Be careful not to touch the patch side which goes on the tube, and once in place press the edges of the patch with a tire spoon.

g) Once the patch appears to be holding well along all edges, pump a very slight amount of air into the tube to avoid wrinkles when it is placed back inside the tire. Put tube in tire; then push the valve stem through the valve stem hole in the rim, and reseat one of the beads. Once one side of the tire—one bead—is back in place, begin reseating the second bead. (Removing all air at this point reduces the chance of a puncture.) In taking off a tire one begins *opposite* the stem; in replacing it one begins work at the stem and works away from it in both directions, being sure to keep the stem pointing straight up. Riders who fail to do this, or who ride with low air pressure in their tires (which causes the tube to shift and the valve stem to angle out of the hole), cause wearing of the stem along its side and base. Once a hole occurs in the valve stem the entire tube is shot, for stems can't hold a patch.

Especially with ATB tires, you might be able to reseat the first bead, and two-thirds or so of the second, without tools. But you'll end up with six inches or so of tire which seems to be far too short to stretch into place. At this point, use your tire spoon in the opposite manner than before—beveled end down.

h) If both beads are properly seated, and the stem is still perpendicular, inflate the tire to its desired pressure. Do this before you put the wheel back on the bike, for it will mean less to mess with if you have goofed with the patch. But don't worry. A chimp can master a patch kit.

i) If the tire remains hard for a minute replace the wheel, tighten axle nuts, re-engage the chain if necessary, and remember to restore your brake's "wire end fixture."

2. Broken spokes/wheel alignment:

This is my least favorite repair and therefore I'm doubly thankful that mountain bike wheels seldom need such work. I've mentioned already that a solid year of daily commuting, trail riding and touring across the country and over all terrains, has not yet required this procedure. Even the finest thin tire wheels would have been destroyed by such treatment. Which means that if you ride conservatively (as I do not) you may *never* need to approach your bike with a spoke wrench in hand.

Let's begin with an analysis of the thin, spindly spoke. If you've never thought of it, ponder for a moment how such slender pillars of metal can hold up the weight of a bike, rider and gear, while being sufficiently light to spin almost effortlessly in circles around a hub. Now look closely at it; a long shank, threads at the top where it screws into the nipple (protruding through the rim hole and holding the spoke in place and under desired tension), and at the other end a right angle crook which holds it in the hub. That sharp bend is the danger point, the place where when stress becomes too great, life ends. It's curtains for the spoke, curses for the rider (who hears that terrible metallic "snap" and prays, as he's coasting to a stop, that the gods have not afflicted him with a freewheel side break), and an opportunity for the spoke wrench to see daylight once again.

More common, however, is a spoke which simply needs adjustment to help re-align (make "true" again) a wheel. Wheels can be out of true in two ways: they can sway from side to side, and they can have high and low spots, which is referred to as being "out of round." Look closely at your wheel. Notice that the spokes reach out to the rim from both sides of the hub. Focus upon one spoke and think what tightening (shortening the length of) that single spoke will do. The rim will be pulled in two directions at the same time when the spoke is tightened, or moved back in two directions if loosened. Tighten the spoke and the rim will be 1) pulled closer to the hub, and 2) pulled in the direction of the side of the hub to which the other end of the spoke is attached. Loosen the spoke and the opposite movement will occur. Tighten a spoke which comes from the other side of the hub and the rim will move in that direction.

"Truing" a wheel is most quickly and successfully accomplished with the wheel off the bike, the tire, tube and rim tape removed, and with the assistance of a truing stand. Such stands have small moveable metal indicators which one slides ever closer to the rim from both sides as the spoke adjustments bring the wheel increasingly into alignment. This can also be done without a stand, using the bike itself to hold the wheel and one's thumb in place of the metal slides. In fact, since spokes break while riding, and because wheels become untrue generally while I'm touring, I've almost always done this repair while far away from home. It's no fun, working on one's bike next to a busy road somewhere. But it *is* better for the wheel than riding with a broken spoke.

Let's pretend you're on your way home from work and hear that snap in your rear hub. (It *will* be your rear hub, unless you've ridden into an open manhole. Rear spokes pack most of the weight.)

a) Stop riding. Push your bike home, call a friend, or fix it—but stop riding. One break brings on another.

b) Remove your commuting bags and water bottle of ammonia, take out your tools and one of the six extra spokes you carry at all times (the nipples taped on the shank, the spokes taped to the seat tube or chainstay tube), and flip your bike onto its back.

c) If you ride home in a necktie, tuck the tail inside your shirt. Otherwise you'll give passing motorists a real treat when they see it get caught in the spokes and strangle you when you spin the wheel to find the tell-tale wobble. Female commuters should think to remove long necklaces, for the same reason.

d) Take off the rear wheel, remove the tire, tube, and rim tape. If the break is on the freewheel side, remove the freewheel (see "freewheel removal" below). Put the wheel back on the bike without tightening axle nuts. (The spoke can be replaced with the wheel off the bike, of course, but I find it much easier to work with when the wheel is back in place; besides, it must be attached again for wheel alignment following spoke replacement.)

e) Remove the broken spoke. This is very easy, for spokes break at the bevel, and can then be taken out by pulling from the nipple end.

f) Take the nipple from the new spoke. Look at the rear hub, and concentrate on the next closest spokes to the one that broke. If you see two spoke heads next to the empty hole in the hub you know that your new spoke must enter from the other side, to follow the alternating pattern around the entire hub. Guide the spoke into the hole. (Don't be afraid to bend the spoke a bit.) Once it is completely through, look at the next closest spoke which enters the hub in the same direction as your replacement spoke. This will be your guide on lacing your replacement—how many spokes you must cross, and which to go over or under with the new spoke. (You'll have to bend the spoke even more here—be sure to bend it along its entire length, thereby not putting a crimp in it.)

g) Put the nipple into the rim, and thread the new spoke into it. Tighten the spoke until it is approximately the same tension as the rest, then align the wheel.

I align wheels with tire, tube, and rim tape removed. This allows for more accurate truing, and exposes the screw head of the spoke nipple for adjustment with a screwdriver. It also allows you to *see* if too much spoke extends through the nipple head—a real danger to the tube. And if the spoke *does* extend too far? This is one reason for buying a Swiss Army knife with a metal file blade. Restore your freewheel to its proper location, and replace your wheel in the frame (if it isn't already there) as it will be when you ride. Tighten axle nuts, but keep the brakes free. Once this is done, follow these steps:

a) Standing behind your wheel, with the bike still on its back, spin the wheel with your hand and note the "wobble," the movement from side to side.

b) Determine the extent of the wobble by placing your thumb next to the wheel rim (with the palm of your hand resting on the chain stay bar), so that your thumbnail lightly touches the rim at every point except for the wobble. At that point the rim will reach out and smack your thumbnail; your job is to pull that wobble back into line with the rest of the rim.

c) Check the tension of the spokes in the area of the wobble. Chances are they'll be a bit more loose than the rest of the spokes in the wheel. Tighten the spoke at the center of the wobble—just a bit at a time, watching its effect upon the rim—then move on to the spokes on either side. (Read the next two steps before proceeding.)

d) But how do you tighten a spoke? And what if two spokes appear to sit right smack in the middle of the problem area? Easy. Just recall that spokes reach out to the rim from both sides of the hub. Naturally, tightening a spoke coming from the right side pulls the rim toward the right; from the left hub side, to the left. If your wobble is to the right, you'll be tightening the spokes which come from the left side of your hub. (I prefer to use a small screwdriver in the nipple slot head—and I always start off with a slight adjustment, about a half-turn for the spoke at wobble center, one-quarter turn for spokes on either side, one-eighth turn for the next two spokes. You can also tighten spokes with a "spoke nipple wrench," but the flat sides on spoke nipples tend to round-off quickly. Therefore, I use the spoke nipple wrench when I am adjusting spokes with the tire still on the rim—something I do only in an emergency.)

e) On occasion you might have to loosen some spokes and tighten others in the wobble area to produce a true wheel, especially if you have trued your wheel several times before. In loosening spokes, follow the same pattern as above; more toward wobble center, less thereafter.

f) When your thumbnail-guide tells you all is well, you have two final things to do. First, check your spokes for approximately the same tension on all. You won't be perfect on this, but at least be close or you'll be aligning your wheel again real soon. Second, step to the side of your bike, spin the wheel and check for its "round." If you have one high spot tighten the spokes slightly in this area—to pull the rim toward the hub a bit. But be sure to watch that you don't lose your side to side true as you do this.

g) I would like to add, as a postscript to wheel alignment, that this has got to be the most exasperating repair work on a bike. Take it easy, and keep your cool.

Bikers use the terms "wobble" and "blip" to denote different problems. "Wobble" is corrected by spoke adjustment, as you have just learned. But "blip" refers to a bulge in the rim wall, a condition which no amount of spoke alignment will eradicate. This problem usually results from riding with tires woefully underinflated, or from riding into huge potholes or sewer drains. Luckily, I've never had a bad blip on my wheels (though I've dealt with more than my share of broken spokes and wheel wobbles). However, on a rough ride through downtown St. Louis my cycling companion once produced a real beauty on the rear wheel of his touring bike. Due to its size he was unable to keep his rear brakes applied when he needed to, for the brake pads touch on the very part of the rim where blips appear. We stopped at a service station to borrow a pair of vise grips, and cut two thin shims of wood from an old paint can stir-stick. We placed these pieces next to the rim, inside the vise grip jaws, then squeezed very carefully. This did the trick for us, but if you someday have a blip which remains on one side of the rim after the other side has been restored, of if a blip has appeared on only one side to begin with, place the wood shim on the flat side, and have a go at the fat blip with the metal jaw of the vise grip. But, squeeze gently, and watch both sides of the rim so that you do not push it past its proper profile.

3. **Bearing maintenance:**

"Sealed" hubs on mountain bikes repel much of the water and road dust which would otherwise enter, but at some point cleaning, inspection and lubrication of wheel bearings is a must. Study the drawing "hub bearings" and you'll see all the component parts, minus the axle nuts and washers and whichever particular "sealed" mechanism your model hub employs. Some are tight-fitting plastic caps, others are metal seals requiring special removal tools for easiest disassembly, with sealed "cartridge" bearing systems inside. (I've not encountered any which can't be removed—albeit less gracefully—with the usual road complement of tools.) Ask your bike shop which kind of sealed hubs they've sold you and where you can obtain the tool.

The only real difference between front and rear wheel bearing maintenance is removal of the freewheel; the following instructions for the front wheel bearings thereby apply to both. See below for freewheel removal procedure.

HUB BEARINGS

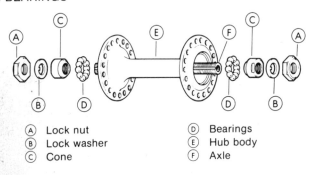

Ⓐ Lock nut	Ⓓ Bearings
Ⓑ Lock washer	Ⓔ Hub body
Ⓒ Cone	Ⓕ Axle

General bearing maintenance steps:

a) Remove the front wheel from the bike and take off the frame-mounting axle nuts and washers.

b) Holding the lock nut on one side of the hub with a crescent wrench or channel locks, use a second wrench to loosen the lock nut on the opposite hub side. Unscrew the lock nut completely, putting it somewhere so that you'll not kick it as you continue working. Next, remove the keyed lock washer. (The term "keyed" is used to denote the small pointed flange of metal on the inside of the washer which fits the groove on the axle.)

c) You are now to the cone, the piece named for its tapering end which rests against the bearings. To adjust the amount of pressure placed on the bearings by this cone the other end of the cone is squared for a "cone wrench"—a very thin wrench which should be used for no other mechanical purpose than that for which it was designed. Take hold of the squared-off end with the cone wrench and back it off the axle completely. (Depending upon the kind of sealed mechanism on your hub, you must now remove—or have already removed—the seal. Study the drawings.)

d) When this is done you have freed one side of the axle, and are free to pull the other axle side out of the hub. Do so, watching for small bearings which might fall out.

e) Now, take a small screwdriver and place the flat edge beneath the dust cap on the hub. This cap is designed to hold the bearings in place, and to fit so snugly into the hub as to keep out most water and dirt. Therefore, it will be difficult to remove, and you may have to lift the cap in several places with the screwdriver before it comes out.

f) With the dust cap gone, look at your bearings (again, if you have the cartridge style seal, you'll have to open the cartridge to see the balls). If you are pulling frequent maintenance there will be grease covering them still; this is a good sign that you have not waited so long that damage to your components might have occurred. Count the bearings, and notice, before you remove them, the small space present—bearings are not supposed to be wedged tightly into place. Now remove the bearings, cleaning and inspecting each individually for pitting and cracks. Bearings cost about a dollar for a bag of twenty or more; a single hub costs from twenty dollars on up. If you save a few cents by keeping cracked or pitted bearings you'll lose dollars in the end with a pitted hub. So replace them when they need it.

Bearing sizes generally fall into the following categories:

3/16"—front hub
1/4"—rear hub, bottom bracket
1/8"—freewheel
5/32"—pedal, headset

g) Once both dust caps and all bearings are removed and cleaned, take out the grease remaining in the hub, and wipe it clean with a cloth. Do the same to the underside of each dust cap. You are now ready to rebuild your wheel.

h) Apply a bead of fresh grease to the bearing cup of one side of your hub. Replace the bearings; then cover them with a second liberal bead of grease. Replace the dust cover by tapping it lightly with the flat side of your 6" crescent wrench.

i) Take the axle (which still has the cone, lockwasher and lock nut on one side) and insert it into the hub side in which you have just replaced the bearings. Be sure to clean and check the cones for they too are far less expensive to replace than an entire hub. Now you can turn your wheel over and replace the bearings in the other side, for the dust cap and cone will keep the bearings from falling out.

j) Once the bearings are in place around the axle on this second side, replace the dust cap, sealed mechanism (its order of replacement will of course depend upon which model you have), and cone—by threading it finger-tight against the bearings. Slide on the lockwasher and screw on the lock nut. Your hub is now rebuilt, but not ready to be ridden, for the cones have not been adjusted to the proper pressure against the bearings. Too loose, and the wheels will roll from side to side, in time ruining your bearings and cup and cone. Too tight, and the wheel will not roll easily.

k) Use the cone wrench to back off the cones a quarter turn or less if when you turn the axle it does not revolve easily in the hub. (The wheel is still off the bike; you should be checking its revolution by hand.) What usually happens is that a person will back off the cones too far, creating side-play. This is when the axle moves back and forth in the hub. Even a slight amount of movement will be greatly accentuated when the wheel is replaced on the frame, so try to remove the side-play while still retaining free rolling movement of the axle. Just when you think you've got the best of both worlds, tighten the lock nuts on both sides. (Hold one side fast, with a crescent wrench or in a vise, while tightening the other side.) The first time you do this you will notice that you have tightened the cone somewhat by snugging the lock nuts—and you'll have to readjust the cone once more. Merely hold the lock nut on one side of the axle with your crescent wrench, while backing off the same side cone ever so slightly with the cone wrench. This is usually sufficient to align it properly, but if not, back off the lock nut a quarter-turn and try again. Expect it to be difficult at first, and much easier the second time.

1) When side-play is absent and the axle moves freely, replace the axle washers and nuts and restore the wheel to the frame. Once it is secured, spin the wheel and check again for rolling ease and for side-play. If it is not correct do not sell your bicycle. Yell or kick the dog, and then return to your bike and adjust your cones once more. But don't give up.

4. Freewheel removal/cleaning:

This was my nemesis on the world ride, more dreaded at times than another bout with food poisoning or dysentery. Seven spokes bit it on that long tour, and of course all were on the freewheel side. This was due to "dishing"—the degree to which the spokes on the right side of the rear wheel are "flattened" (run from the rim to the hub at a straighter angle than the left side) to allow for the freewheel space on the axle. There were no pocket vises back then, and the freewheel tool I packed along turned out to be made of brass—not steel. It fell apart when I needed it just east of Munich; it was pure improvisation after that.

But you won't have that hassle, for bikes have come a long way. And with the stronger rims, thick spokes and greatly reduced dishing of ATB wheels, you'll probably only remove your freewheel to pull maintenance.

STANDARD HUB AND FREEWHEEL

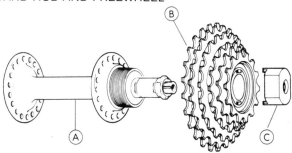

Ⓐ   Hub body
Ⓑ   Freewheel
Ⓒ   Freewheel tool

When you buy your bike, ask which kind of freewheel puller (removal tool) you'll need, and purchase it. Then follow these steps for disassembly:

a) If you have access to a large vise, clamp the flattened sides of the removal tool tightly in its jaws. Remove the rear wheel, take off axle nuts and washers, and lay the wheel on top of the tool—being sure that the removal tool's splines or notches engage the freewheel properly.

b) Now take hold of the wheel at the 3 o'clock and 9 o'clock positions, and turn the wheel counterclockwise. A fair amount of force—especially if you're a strong rider—must be applied before you'll feel the freewheel give way. Continue to spin the wheel counterclockwise until it separates from the freewheel; you can then lift off the wheel and unscrew the cluster by hand through its last few threads.

c) If a large vise isn't present, and you're on the road, you have the option of the pocket vise (or, if you've forgotten it, gripping your freewheel tool with the small 7" channel locks, wrapping a bungie around the handles and straining for all you're worth). But if you're home, or can find a garage while on tour, it's time for the huge 15" crescent. A pipe wrench works in a pinch, but provides a far less sure grip on the freewheel tool.

d) Place the removal tool in the crescent's jaws as tightly as possible. Stand over your wheel, the freewheel on the right, your left hand at the top of your rim. Engage the removal tool and freewheel securely, and position the wheel so that the wrench handle angles up toward you, not away from you. Take hold of the wrench and push down on it, being careful not to allow the removal tool to slip out of the freewheel. With the application of a good deal of pressure the freewheel will "break," and then you can easily thread it off the wheel.

e) Upon removing the freewheel a plastic or metal spoke protector will be encountered. Slip it off; the spoke holes in the hub can now be seen, and bearing maintenance can be pulled just as with the front hub.

(Replace the freewheel by reversing removal directions above.)

Clean the freewheel core by taking the freewheel off the wheel and laying it upside down (smallest sprocket to the ground) on newspaper. Then flush the core with Liquid Wrench. This is done by shooting the liquid between the dust ring and main body of the core—just inside the sprocket on the back side. Give the Liquid Wrench a few minutes to work through the bearings. Spin the freewheel several times and move it to a dry piece of paper, then flush it again. (If the ball bearings inside the core were dirty the first newspaper will be dark with grease.) A third flushing may be necessary. Then allow the bearings to dry for a few minutes, and apply a fine, light bicycle oil.

5. Freewheel Disassembly:

If a sprocket has worn out, or you wish to alter your gear ratios, the freewheel must be broken down into its component parts of body, spacers and sprockets. (The body can itself be disassembled, but I would do this only if you make watches for a living.) The job may be done with the cluster on or off the wheel, but I find it much easier when separate. Follow the instructions above for freewheel removal.

You'll need one sprocket tool (a long steel rod with a piece of chain riveted to one end) if you have access to a good shop vise, two tools if you do not.

a) When using two sprocket tools, place the chain of one tool around the fourth sprocket down (second to largest), wrapping the chain in a clockwise direction. Notice that the tools have a device (on the same rod end as the chain, but opposite side) to engage the sprocket and hold fast between the teeth; this device should be engaged and pointed in the direction you wish to turn that particular sprocket.

SPROCKET TOOLS

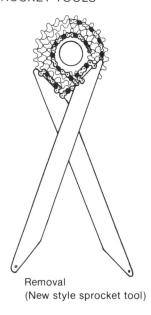

Removal
(New style sprocket tool)

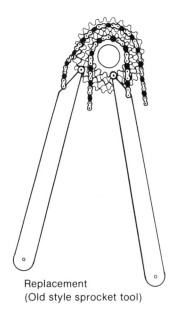

Replacement
(Old style sprocket tool)

(A second kind of sprocket tool is now available. In place of a rivet tip, this tool has a short length of chain, plus the longer one. The grip is more secure, the handles are crossed and pushed toward one another for disassembly. Follow the directions which come with these tools.)

b) In the opposite direction wrap the chain of the second tool around the first (smallest) cogwheel. Place these tools so that the handles are only a few inches apart. This allows greater control, for the handles must be pushed toward one another to unscrew the top sprocket. A strong rider's freewheel will require a great deal of strength to disassemble, for the first two sprockets are actually tightened on the freewheel body during pedalling. (When you are using two sprocket tools be careful not to apply uneven pressure against the handles, for this will cause the entire freewheel to tilt and your tools will slip off.) On most freewheels the first two sprockets screw off the freewheel body or core in a counterclockwise direction, and the three remaining cogwheels lift off. These last three have small lugs which fit the notches in the core, and usually have spacer rings between them. Don't get the sequence mixed up when you take things apart—with a freewheel you must also replace the sprockets with the same side up as you found them.

c) There are two ways to disassemble a cluster if you have access to a vise. The first is to grip the largest sprocket in the vise (the freewheel is standing up), wrap the sprocket tool chain around the first (smallest) cogwheel in a counterclockwise direction, and apply force. Remove the second in the same manner, and then proceed as above.

d) The second method requires an inexpensive "freewheel-axle vise tool," which holds the cluster in a horizontal position for the easiest of all disassemblies.

CHAPTER TWELVE

BOTTOM BRACKETS

As you have gathered by now, most parts of a bike have more than one name. So it is in this section, which includes the crank assembly of chainwheels (chainrings), the cranks (crankarms), and bottom bracket spindle (axle). But you won't be confused if you study your bike, the drawings, and proceed slowly.

Take a close look at the entire assembly. I normally pull maintenance on bracket bearings without ever touching the right side of this system—the side with chainrings. Why? Because it's far easier and faster to remove only the left side crank, lock ring and adjustable cup, and take out the right side bearings by reaching through the short bottom bracket. Most people who have trouble with this maintenance experience it with cotter pins (I haven't seen a mountain bike with them yet; all models have the easily removed *cotterless* cranks), or when trying to back out the ride side "fixed" cup. I will, however, go through the steps necessary to remove all pieces, and you can decide for yourself how you wish to reach your bearings.

CRANKSET

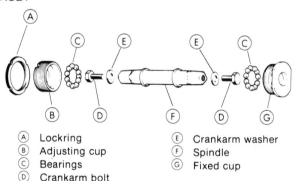

(A) Lockring
(B) Adjusting cup
(C) Bearings
(D) Crankarm bolt
(E) Crankarm washer
(F) Spindle
(G) Fixed cup

98

TOURING CRANKSET

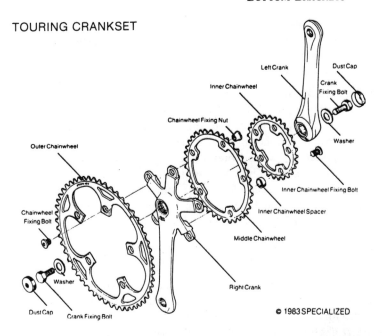

© 1983 SPECIALIZED

One further point before we begin. As with wheels, several companies have different kinds of "sealed" mechanisms on their crank hubs. Some employ the less sophisticated (though effective) "O" rings alone, some have O-rings and tight-fitting plastic dust covers, and some have cover assemblies plus shields or sleeves or fully enclosed bearing "cassettes" inside the hubs. None of these are particularly difficult to work with, and should not be beyond anyone who can follow the general directions provided for maintenance. Merely deal with your particular seal whenever it appears in the assembly/disassembly sequence, and ask your bike dealer for replacement O-rings and cassettes. (While it's good to have replacements on hand, I've re-used these many times.)

1. Chainring removal/disassembly
2. Bottom bracket disassembly
3. Bottom bracket reassembly

1. **Chainring removal/disassembly:**

a) Begin by removing the two small plastic or metal crankarm dust caps; throw them over your left shoulder for good luck. No, this isn't superstition. It's just a good way to insure that you'll never have these pieces freeze up on you out on the road. Their value is almost all aesthetic, and while I've had problems with both the metal and plastic kind, I've never had any difficulties when neither were present. (Both kinds screw out of the crankarm counterclockwise.)

b) The crankarm fixing bolts are now exposed. Universal tools have sprocket-type heads fitted for the various sizes of bolts; crank tools made specifically for one type of crank will have one end which fits the crankarm bolt, and the other end either bevelled to accept the jaws of a larger crescent, or a short breaker bar assembly to twist off the bolt. Remove the crankarm bolt (let's assume we're working with the right-chainring-side), and *don't* forget to remove the washer as well. Fail to pull out the washer and the next step will not work. (Crankarm bolts on both sides are removed counterclockwise.)

c) Screw the crankarm puller into the crankarm as far as it will go, making sure that the threads mesh perfectly.

d) Now insert the extractor portion—that piece which turns through the inside of the puller—into the puller body; turn it by hand until you feel its tip engage the spindle (axle) end. With a breaker bar, crescent or universal tool turn the extractor; you will see the chainring assembly begin to slide toward you, away from and off the spindle. Lift the chain off the chainring, place it out of the way on the bottom bracket housing, and remove the left side crankarm in the same manner.

e) This is an excellent time to clean your chainring, check your pedals, and make sure the "chainring fixing bolts"—those which hold the sprockets together, located near the spider—are tight. These seldom come loose, but if they do they'll produce an untrue chainring, and cause chain rub and noise on the front derailleur cage. The individual chainrings can be separated easily by using an allen wrench to remove these fixing bolts, and lifting off the rings.

2. **Bottom bracket disassembly:**

a) Once the crankarms are removed, you can proceed to the bottom bracket. As I mentioned, I remove only the left side adjustable cup, but the fixed cup can be removed with a lock ring/fixed cup tool—counterclockwise.

b) On tour, under duress, one can bang away with a screwdriver or punch and hammer to remove the lockring and adjustable cup. But you'll destroy your lock ring this way; besides, you shouldn't need to mess with your bottom bracket on tour unless it's an especially arduous ride. Using the proper tool—the lock ring/fixed cup tool—engage the angled tip in the lock ring notch, and remove it—counterclockwise. Now use an adjustable cup tool to engage the "pin holes" in the cup's face, and back it out completely.

c) The ball bearings will probably be in a retainer. If so, notice in which direction the retainer faces as you remove the spindle. You can see in the drawing that the solid back of the retainer faces *away* from you. Also, notice if one end of the spindle is longer than the other. If it is, the longer side will extend toward the chainwheels. Clean, inspect, and if necessary replace all bearings. Wipe all surfaces clean, and also inspect the spindle and cups for bearing wear. (See appendix E.)

3. **Bottom bracket reassembly:**

a) Apply a generous bead of grease on the inside of your fixed cup, replace the bearings, and cover them with a second layer of grease. Now thread this cup back into the frame (right side, chainring side), snugging it well. To insure easy removal some months in the future, always apply a bit of grease to the threads inside the bottom bracket before replacing the cups.

b) Lubricate and replace the bearings in the adjustable cup in the same manner, but do not yet thread the cup into place.

c) Take the cleaned spindle, longer side toward the fixed cup, and, from the other side of the bike (left side) carefully guide it through the bracket and fixed cup.

d) While holding the spindle end in one hand, pick up the adjustable cup, engage the spindle in the cup hole, and thread it into the frame. Stop threading this cup when it engages the bearings, and check for side-play in the spindle. If it is present, thread the cup a bit further, but not so far as to prohibit the free turning of the spindle.

e) When the adjustment is correct replace the lock ring, then re-check for proper bearing adjustment. As with wheels, this can be troubling until you get the hang of it, for the lock ring can budge the adjustable cup a bit and throw you off. Have patience.

f) Replace both crankarms by slipping them onto the spindle, and tightening the fixing bolts. These must be well-secured, and should be checked for tightness once every forty or fifty miles for the next two hundred miles. Re-engage the chain on the chainring, and you're ready to roll.

CHAPTER THIRTEEN

BRAKES

I've found brakes on ATBs to be similar in this respect to the mountain bike in general: maintenance is seldom required, is usually minor, and the size and nature of the component makes repairs easy to understand and perform.

1. brake lever position/cable replacement
2. brake pad maintenance

CANTILEVER BRAKE

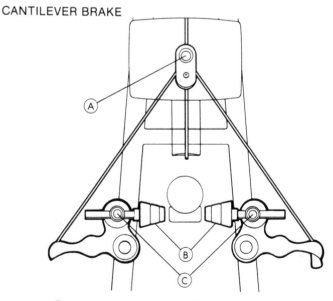

Ⓐ Cable anchor bolt   Ⓒ Brake shoe anchor nuts
Ⓑ Brake shoes

1. Brake lever position/Cable replacement:

Look closely at the entire brake assembly, from lever to cables to hook links and pads. (See Shimano brake illustration in appendix.) The drawings should make the purpose of each piece clear, but we'll go through it to be sure. Also, each brand of mountain brakes has slight differences, but these should be of no difficulty whatsoever if you pay close attention to all pieces during disassembly.

a) The brake lever's position on the handlebars can be changed very easily. An allen wrench is all that's necessary to loosen the "lever fixing bolt," re-position and tighten. (Be sure on all brake repairs that you check your work several times before you ride.)

b) If you break a cable remove the old one and screw down (*into* the lever body) the fixing nut and outer cable adjusting bolt. Cables stretch in time; if this adjusting bolt is returned to its original position with each new cable it will be able to take up the slack produced over time. (When the time comes screw out the adjusting bolt, and lock it in position by cinching the fixing nut tightly against it.)

c) Remove the old cable from the cable housing, grease the new cable and slide it through the housing; be sure to replace the "outer cable end cap." (Shimano brakes have a small "inner cable end adapter" through which the new cable must be threaded *before* it is run through the housing.) Insert the round "inner cable end" into the brake handle, line up the grooves in the fixing nut and outer cable adjusting bolt, push the cable into these slots, and trap it in place by cinching the outer cable end cap into the outer cable adjusting bolt.

Are these huge names for tiny pieces getting to you? Don't become upset; just follow along on the drawings and realize it takes longer to read about this than to do the repair a *second* time. The laborious detail in description is only to insure that you won't be confused the first time you tackle repairs.

d) Remove the "cable carrier" from the old cable, slip it onto the new cable and gauge its approximate location by pulling up on the "center wire" until the brake pads almost touch the rim. Now remove the center wire from the cable carrier without changing the carrier's position, and tighten. Push the "hook link" toward the rim to disengage the "wire end fixture," use the slack produced to replace the center wire in the cable carrier, push the hook link toward the rim again and affix the wire end fixture.

e) Squeeze the brake handle a few times very hard, check to see that all is connected properly, and that the brake pads are resting only 2mm (between 1/16" and 1/8") from the rim. Spin the wheel and look for any rubbing of rim against pad. You'll have to true the wheel if you can't keep the brakes close to the rim without the pads rubbing. (Some riders simply adjust more slack into the cable, but this is dangerous in that it increases one's reaction time in braking, while decreasing braking power.)

f) When all seems fine, leave about 1-1½" of cable extending past the cable carrier, cut off the surplus, and either solder or crimp a protective cap over the end.

2. Brake pad maintenance:

Proper pad position can be a confusing thing to discuss, due to the number of possible directional movements. Look at the assembly: the pad must strike the rim with its entire face (rotation, height), it must be closer to the rim at one end than the other (angle), and the pads must both rest close to and equidistant from the rim (clearance).

a) Begin by checking the link fixing bolts. Tighten them until there is no swaying of the calipers; all caliper movement should be either toward or away from the rim. (As suggested in Part One for fender stay mounting bolts which might continue to come loose, a drop of "Loc-Tight" will keep an intransigent bolt in place.)

b) Look at the backside of each brake shoe (the metal holder for the pad). The longer of the three holes must point away from the bike—toward the front for front brakes, toward the rear for rear brakes. (Some models will have slightly different index systems.) This actually "toes in" or angles the more forward end of all pads toward the rims, for maximum stopping power. Observe brake shoe hole placement *before* you remove the old pads.

c) There is no need to remove control and wave washers when replacing pads, but if you do be sure to replace everything exactly as before—in both sequence and correct front/back side. Use the drawings, lay out the pieces in order as they come off, and don't take all four pad assemblies apart at the same time.

d) To replace pads without taking things apart, first release the wire end fixture from the hook link; both links will fall back into a resting position which is far easier to work with than when they're under tension from the center wire and close to the rim. Next, hold the brake shoe fixing nut fast with a crescent or channel locks. Loosen the allen head brake shoe fixing bolt until the "brake shoe fixing pin" moves freely.

e) Slip out the old shoe and slip in the new, with the long hole on its back pointing away from the bike. Tighten the brake shoe fixing bolt and nut so that movement is still possible by hand when you rotate the control washer, or similar device on other models, but not so loose that it moves by itself. Replace all pads in this manner, and re-engage the wire end fixture and hook link.

f) Now adjust the control washer A (or similar device) so as to gain the proper pad angle (see drawing). Rotate and move toward or away from the rim the brake shoe fixing pin until height, rotation, and equidistant clearance of pads is attained.

g) Tighten all brake shoe fixing bolts and nuts, re-check all pad positions, and place a drop or spray of light lubricant on the pivot points of the brake lever and caliper links.

CHAPTER FOURTEEN

PEDALS

I find few riders who service their pedal bearings until a squeak develops. They invariably suspect the bottom bracket first, and move on to the pedal as a last resort. For some reason these components suffer amazing neglect.

They do, however, hold up very well under this abuse. And the beautiful, sealed bear traps found on better ATBs can really take a beating. But don't push it. Maintenance on pedals is much like working with wheel hubs (except that a pedal is between the cones), and is much easier.

1. bearing maintenance

PEDAL

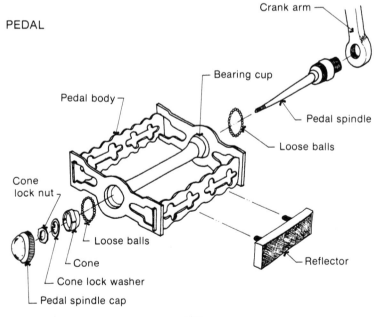

1. **Bearing maintenance:**

a) It is easiest to work on bearings if the oval, outer pedal guard (not present on all pedals) is removed. This requires a very small allen wrench. A larger allen is then needed to remove the pedal spindle cap, which exposes the cone lock nut, washer, cone and bearings inside. (Maintenance can be pulled with the pedal on or off the bike. Remove the pedals with a thin crescent, a specific-purpose pedal wrench, or—most easily if your brand is so fitted—an allen wrench applied to the back of the pedal axle.)

b) Remove the lock nut and keyed washer, exposing the cone.

c) Due to the pedal housing you cannot get a wrench on the cone; the cone therefore has slots cut in its side (the side facing you) for your screwdriver. Using a small screwdriver blade, back the cone off the spindle.

d) Remove the cone, catching all the bearings. Slip off the pedal, clean, inspect, and lubricate the bearings, bearing cups, and cones on both sides.

e) Reassemble. Adjust cone for proper pressure against bearings in the same manner as described in wheel maintenance—free rotation of pedal but no side-play.

f) Replace the outer pedal guard.

CHAPTER FIFTEEN

CHAINS

Road grime, trail mud and rainwater all attack from the outside, while internally—especially on tour—the strain of pedalling with such weight stretches the metal links. For efficient, quiet cycling you've *got* to service this component.

1. frozen links and disassembly
2. cleaning
3. chain reassembly
4. determining chain length

1. Frozen links and disassembly:

a) The chain consists of many individual links, each made up of metal side plates, small bars called "rollers" to engage the teeth of sprockets, and tiny rivets to hold the side plates and rollers together. Metal side plates of successive links rub on one another, and rollers must spin upon the rivets as they move around the chainwheel and cluster. All this metal upon metal contact—times a hundred links or so—should make it obvious that a lubricant must always be at hand. On tour I pack a small plastic bottle of oil, but for around town and especially trail riding (where the dust readily adheres to all oiled surfaces) I use spray "dri-lube," a non-petroleum synthetic lubricant. When I do use oil I put only a drop on each roller, rub the entire chain with a lightly oiled cloth, turn the cranks a few times and wait several minutes for the lubricant to penetrate past the rivets. Then I wipe the chain with a dry cloth, for any *visible* oil won't do you any good.

b) You'll need a "chain rivet tool" to free frozen links and for disassembly. (And you'll also need to look at it carefully while going through these instructions.) When a link becomes frozen, it is often caused by dryness, and makes itself known by jumping over teeth in the sprockets, or by causing the rear derailleur to jerk forward suddenly as it passes over the jockey and tension pulleys. Elevate your rear wheel and turn the crank to find the culprit link, and when you do, coat it with a light oil and work the link with your fingers. This may free it. If it doesn't, you'll have to use the chain tool.

c) When viewed from the side, the chain tool looks like a wide "U," with two shorter "walls" of metal between. Place the tool in front of you with the handle to the right side. Twist the handle counterclockwise to remove the rivet "pin" from view. Now, take your chain, or preferably a few old links for practice first (many bike shops have old ones lying around which they'll give you), and place it over the first of these inner walls from the right side. It will usually be somewhat wider than the left-hand wall. Notice, when you view your chain tool from the top, that these walls have an open space in the middle, and the chain roller rests in it with the "plates" on either side of the wall. To free a frozen link it should be placed in just this manner on the right-hand wall. Turn the tool handle clockwise until the tool rivet pin touches the chain rivet. As you turn the handle more, notice how the plates move slightly farther apart. Most often only the slightest rivet adjustment is necessary to free the link. Be sure not to push the rivet flush with the side plate, for its length is such that it should extend slightly past the plates on both sides. If it is necessary to push the rivet flush to free the link, simply turn the chain over in the tool and apply pressure against the opposite end of the rivet.

d) To remove the chain it is necessary to drive a rivet out of one side plate past the roller, yet still leave the rivet held in place in the far side plate. This last part is the killer, and you should practice it a few times at home before having to do it on the road. (I have twice accidentally driven the rivet completely free of the second plate; the first time I luckily had extra links around, the second time I did not. It took me a good half hour to wedge the free rivet back into the side plate, using the chain tool and my needlenose pliers.) Place the chain over the left-hand wall of your chain tool, and turn the handle clockwise until the tool rivet pin touches the chain rivet. Some bike shop mechanics will tell you to then turn the handle six times without fear. This is supposed to place the rivet beyond the roller, but still in the far side plate. Perhaps they suggest this so nonchalantly because bike shops use a special pliers-like tool which in one quick squeeze of the handles pushes the rivet out to the exact desired spot. For me, it's touch and go past the fifth handle turn. Beyond that I make a quarter-turn and pull on the chain to see if it will fall free, then another quarter-turn and another tug, and so on. (I've recently seen advertised a chain tool like the bike shops use, but small and inexpensive. The manufacturer guarantees its use with all chain types, and says it ends the worry about pushing the rivet out of the far side plate. You might look for this, but compare its size and weight to the regular tool if you'll be carrying it on tour.)

2. Cleaning:

Once the chain is free from the bike soak it in a solvent of kerosene or gasoline, working all links and brushing the dirtiest plates with a wire brush. Then suspend the chain from a nail to dry for a half-hour, and wipe away any remaining solvent with a cloth. Lubricate as above.

On a ride to Yellowstone in '76 I met a man who explained how he melted paraffin blocks, dipped his chain, and *never* had to worry about dirty oil or grease accumulation. I tried it, but didn't care for the hassle of melting the paraffin, the relatively short time between required dippings, and the fact that I couldn't simply add a touch of oil when developing a squeak on the road.

3. Chain Reassembly:

Replace the chain on the bike so that the extended rivet faces you; otherwise you'll be trying to use the chain tool backwards. When you have driven the rivet back through the roller and into the second plate you'll probably find the link to be stiff. If you do, place the link on the right-hand plate and free it, following the directions above.

4. Determining chain length:

Once you know that you do need another chain (when you have an inch or more of lateral play, causing noise and sloppy pedalling and shifting), count the number of links in your old one, and buy a new chain with exactly that number. But, should you need to fit a chain to your bike and for some reason you can't determine or trust the old length, follow this procedure. (It is not the easiest method, but is in my opinion the most exact.) Put your new chain on the largest sprockets in front and rear. This should just about pull your rear derailleur cage until it is parallel with the chainstay. Give it some assistance by pulling the chain taut if needed, then lift the chain at the top of the chainwheel. You should have between one-half and one full link of extra chain at this point.

*   *   *

I hate to end a book with a cold discussion of repairs. It's like giving blood—you know you *should* do it—without getting the warm smile, cold juice and big cookie at the end.

So let this short page be my warm smile to you. You deserve it—*anyone* who has waded through the chilling mechanical abyss of Part Two, and who now intends to care properly for his mount—deserves it.

Happy trails, happy touring, and happy city travel to you all.

APPENDICES

APPENDIX A

Gear Chart for 26″ Wheel

Number of teeth in front sprocket

	24	26	28	30	32	34	36	38	40	42	44	46	48	50	52
12	52	56.3	60.7	65	69.3	73.4	78	82.3	86.7	91	95.3	99.7	104	108.3	112.7
13	48	52	56	60	64	68	72	76	80	84	88	92	96	100	104
14	44.6	48.3	52	55.8	59.4	63.1	66.9	70.6	74.3	78	81.7	85.4	89.1	92.9	96.6
15	41.6	45.1	48.5	52	55.5	58.9	62.4	65.9	69.3	72.8	76.3	79.7	83.2	86.7	90.1
16	39	42.3	45.5	48.8	52	55.3	58.5	61.8	65	68.3	71.5	74.8	78	81.3	84.5
17	36.7	39.8	42.8	45.9	48.9	52	55.1	58.1	61.2	64.2	67.3	70.4	73.4	76.5	79.5
18	34.7	37.6	40.4	43.3	46.2	49.1	52	54.9	57.8	60.7	63.6	66.4	69.3	72.2	75.1
19	32.8	35.6	38.3	41.1	43.8	46.5	49.3	52	54.7	57.8	60.2	62.9	65.7	68.4	71.2
20	31.2	33.8	36.4	39	41.6	44.2	46.8	49.4	52	54.6	57.2	59.8	62.4	65	67.6
21	29.7	32.2	34.7	37.1	39.6	42.1	44.6	47	49.5	52	54.5	57	59.4	61.9	63.4
22	28.4	30.7	33.1	35.5	37.8	40.2	42.5	44.9	47.3	49.6	52	54.4	56.7	59.1	61.5
23	27.1	29.4	31.7	33.9	36.2	38.4	40.7	43	45.2	47.5	49.7	52	54.3	56.5	58.8
24	26	28.2	30.3	32.5	34.7	36.8	39	41.2	43.3	45.5	47.7	49.8	52	54.2	56.3
25	25	27	29.1	31.2	33.3	35.4	37.4	39.5	41.6	43.7	45.8	47.8	49.9	52	54.1
26	24	26	28	30	32	34	36	38	40	42	44	46	48	50	52
27	23.1	25	27	28.9	30.8	32.7	34.7	36.6	38.5	40.4	42.4	44.3	46.2	48.1	50.1
28	22.3	24.1	26	27.9	29.7	31.6	33.4	35.3	37.1	39	40.9	42.7	44.6	46.4	48.3
29	21.5	23.3	25.1	26.9	28.7	30.5	32.3	34.1	35.9	37.7	39.4	41.2	43	44.8	46.6
30	20.8	22.5	24.3	26	27.7	29.5	31.2	32.9	34.7	36.4	38.1	39.9	41.6	43.3	45.1
31	20.1	21.8	23.5	25.2	26.8	28.5	30.2	31.9	33.5	35.2	36.9	38.6	40.3	41.9	43.6
32	19.5	21.1	22.8	24.4	26	27.6	29.3	30.9	32.5	34.1	35.8	37.4	39	40.6	42.3
33	18.9	20.5	22.1	23.6	25.2	26.7	28.4	29.9	31.5	33.1	34.7	36.2	37.8	39.4	41
34	18.4	19.9	21.4	22.9	24.5	26	27.5	29.1	30.6	32.1	33.6	35.2	36.7	38.2	39.8
35	17.8	19.3	20.8	22.3	23.8	25.3	26.7	28.2	29.7	31.2	32.7	34.2	35.7	37.1	38.6
36	17.3	18.8	20.2	21.7	23.1	24.6	26	27.4	28.9	30.3	31.8	33.2	34.7	36.1	37.6

Number of teeth in rear sprocket (left axis)

inch gear $= \dfrac{\text{\# teeth in front sprocket}}{\text{\# teeth in rear sprocket}} \times$ wheel diameter in inches

Example: $\dfrac{48}{13} \times 26 = 96$ inch gear

(Compute linear distance traveled with each crank rotation by multiplying "inch gear" by pi = 3.14)

Example: $96 \times 3.14 = 301.44″$ (or 25.12′ linear distance)

APPENDIX B

Direct your written enquiries about federal lands to the following offices:

BUREAU OF LAND MANAGEMENT
U. S. Department of the Interior
18th and "C" Streets, N.W.
Room 1013
Washington, D. C. 20240

NATIONAL FORESTS AND WILDERNESS AREAS
Forest Service
U. S. Department of Agriculture
12th and Independence Streets, S.W.
P. O. Box 2417
Washington, D. C. 20013

NATIONAL PARKS AND RELATED AREAS
National Park Service
U. S. Department of the Interior
18th and "C" Streets, N.W.
Room 1013
Washington, D. C. 20240

APPENDIX C

Addresses of Manufacturers Encountered in the Text

Below are listed the mailing addresses of manufacturers whose products are discussed in the text. It is important when corresponding with these companies to be very specific in your requests for information. Most are anxious to be of help, so make it easy for them by telling them exactly what you have, and what you want. Also included in this appendix is a detailed discussion of a number of different panniers. Like all product comparisons in this book, the goal is to point out what things *you* should consider before making a purchase, rather than to advocate a particular line or product.

First, a note on testing procedures. I spend months on the road each year, following historic trails, riding specific areas for articles, pedalling states for bicycle guides. All this time spent in the saddle provides a perfect opportunity to test equipment under exactly those conditions for which it is designed. Because I tour year-round I have a chance to see if cold makes some parts brittle, if day-long rains have an effect, if constant sun will bleach out colors or cause leather to crack.

When I'm touring with others we often exchange panniers. And when on extended solo rides I mail equipment to a town halfway along the trail, transfer my gear into new packs, and thereby test competitors. The average rider, still wincing at the cost of his bags, will treat them very gingerly. My situation is quite different, and though I'm not brutal with the gear, I do not baby it. Rough use comes with the territory.

Finally, you won't find much technical reporting in my notes. I seldom count the number of stitches per inch, or concentrate on how a bag is sewn; poor construction will make itself evident soon enough.

Lone Peak:

These panniers are made of tough 11.5 ounce Cordura nylon, and are coated throughout with an effective WaterLok waterproof coating. (That is, it's effective for all but torrential storms; somehow moisture finds its way into *any* bag without a raincover.) Stainless steel hardware is employed, the bags are held together with allen head screws and nyloc nuts (instead of rivets; repairs are thus much easier), and the stiffeners are made of smooth-edged ABS (the tough, light material used in kayaks). Two large exterior pockets—one in the main compartment closing flap, the second a long vertical enclosure at the rear of the bag—are closed with tough, self-repairing coil zippers, made even easier to use due to pull tabs at both ends. A horizontal compression strap is present; it and the two vertical cinch straps which reach up to the top flap are connected by quick, convenient "Fastex" side release ladder-loc buckles. The top pocket flap has two lash-tabs, to aid in carrying fishing poles or other items, while the main compartment inside is further protected from moisture and dust by a waterproof nylon taffeta with a drawstring closure on top. (The Cordura bag top also has a drawstring closure, making the main compartment triple-sealed.) As with Lone Peak touring bags, a convenient map pocket sits high against the back wall of each pannier.

These bags mount *very* easily. An "S" hook attached to a bottom tension strap is first engaged; the bag is then pulled up and onto the rack, resting on the uncoated double wrap stainless steel hooks. (D-rings sit next to each hook as attachment points for extra gear or shoulder strap.) Finally, a nylon web strap located at the top rear center of the pannier is wrapped beneath the top rack support, and secured by a DuPont "Delrin" buckle. (This web strap is unnecessary while commuting, unless one hops curbs with esprit.) When off the bike the bags can be snapped together and transported by shoulder straps or built-in handle. As mentioned in Chapter Three, these bags can now be turned into backpacks with a "conversion back pad."

I found the Lone Peak system—handlebar bag, huge rear panniers and smaller front bags (identical to rear except in size)—to be extremely durable. Overloaded with water weight on my Utah desert ride, I again burdened these bags for a winter mountain run when I toured alone. I was forced to pack a great amount of heavy gear for that cold tour, and it took its toll. In both rear panniers that ABS stiffener—to which the mounting hooks are attached—ripped at the rear hook point. (This is a simple repair, however; the allen head screws are backed out of their nyloc nuts, the stiffener slipped out of the bag and replaced.) This was the single problem in construction; all seams, zippers, tension points held firm. *Note: The stiffeners have now been replaced by an even higher density material, designed not to tear or crack when abused.

I've already mentioned (Chapter Three) that the handlebar bag does not have a map case; this was sorely missed. I also found the two straps and buckles which close off the main compartment of the panniers to be one too many. No doubt two were chosen to attain a better seal of this top flap against the elements (Lone Peak does not use an elasticized hood like Kirtland and Kangaroo; thus two are needed), but with the many times on tour when access is desirable a *double* strap system is cumbersome. This is, however, an extremely minor point, as the Fastex side release buckles release and re-engage as fast as one can squeeze the plastic buckle sides and pull. Still, it was commented upon by two of three test riders, who preferred the single strap system of Kirtland and Kangaroo, and the zipper entry into Madden and Needle Works bags.

But the major problem I had with these bags is an element of design shared by every mountain and touring bike pannier I've tested, except for Needle Works and Madden. That difficulty is the hassle of access to top-loading rear panniers while a bike is fully loaded. One's tent, pad and sleeping bag rest horizontally upon the rack; this means that they extend directly over the top of the panniers (a problem made still worse if one completely fills the top flap pockets). The front-loading Needle Works panniers are an answer to this problem, and do not possess the troubles of side-loading bags (in which gear is difficult to reach and falls out easily). If you seldom reach into rear panniers during the day, however, or do not travel as fully loaded as I, the top-loading design will cause no trouble.

Kirtland:

This company's off-road "Blazer Packs" are a sharp looking system of handlebar bag (with map case—Chapter Three), "Rack Pack" (Chapter Three), and large front and rear panniers; all but the handlebar bag come with "Scotchlite" reflective striping. Made of abrasion-resistant 11 ounce Cordura (Waterlok-treated against rain), the packs have top flap and rear pockets like Lone Peak and use similar quality materials and care in construction. A drawstring closure of nylon taffeta protects the main compartment, with the elasticized top flap pocket (serving as a "dust and mud collar") fitting snugly over that. This is held closed by a single vertical nylon strap with Fastex side release buckle; two horizontal compression straps serve to hold gear close to the frame.

But these bags differ most of all in their radical departure from the normal hook-and-spring or strap-and-velcro mounting systems. In place of these is a "Leverlok," an injection molded nylon lever which clamps its rubber head against a rack's top tube. Beneath this lever is a triangular nylon "Sway Guard" plate, which houses a double lower hook and its elastic strap, and protects the pack material from rack abrasion. The rider merely engages the lower hook to the lower rack brace, then lifts and rests the bag upon the rack by means of two nylon-coated hooks. He then reaches behind the bag for the leverlok handle, and snaps it into place.

I must admit I wasn't much impressed when I first viewed this mounting system at the Las Vegas International Bike Show. It appeared so insubstantial; I assumed it would work well enough in easy terrain, but I doubted it would hold when things got rough. And sure enough, our first day out on a rough November Utah ride one of the bags fell off.

We stopped and sat amongst the desert scrub to study things a bit. Had it been mounted properly? Had the rubber tip worked loose? (I had been sent a set of early prototypes to test; later production models have this rubber block set far more permanently in place.) Was the locking plate adjusted for the rack? (A tiny pocket inside the bag contains the necessary allen wrench.) All seemed okay, until I asked my friend to mount the bag exactly as he had before. In doing so he noticed that he hadn't paid particular attention to snapping the lever in place. This is easily accomplished (though one must reach between the wheel and bag to grab the lever; large hands might find this cumbersome at first), but none of us had worked with them before. A quick investigation showed that a second pack on the bike was also mounted incorrectly. We corrected the error and rode without incident thereafter. (And with no problem on two later trips as well.)

Another feature I should mention on these packs is the manner in which the top mounting hooks (which hang over the rack supporting the bag's weight) are attached to the panniers. Although done so with rivets which are difficult to fix if there's a breakdown on the road, they are attached to a strong, light sheet of 6061-T6 aircraft grade aluminum. Loaded heavily and abused, there was not a single sign of stress along the rivets, seam, or leverlok.

The bags snap together when off the bike, and can be carried by a single leather handle. However, there are no D-rings for carrying by shoulder strap (an extremely minor matter to me, as I *never* carry my panniers this way), and no facility to turn the bag into a backpack. This second drawback is of more importance to me, as I like this option for some off-bike hands-free climbing. (I'll be surprised if every company doesn't offer such a system soon.)

Kangaroo:

What a selection! This company has a line of mountain bike packs and accessories which make shopping tremendous fun, and hard riding easier. A "Portage Pad" of ensolite velcroes around the top and seat tubes for less painful shoulder transports of your bike. The "Klunker Frame Bagg" velcroes to the down and top tubes, providing 175 cubic inches of storage space inside the frame triangle. Double handlebar bags can be mounted; the "Moosebag" on top, the "Sonora" or larger "Tioga" (with map case) bags in front. A "Mountain Tool Kit Bagg" is designed to velcro anywhere there's frame room free, and a "Mountain Stuff Sac" with a rear triangle of "Scotchlite" reflective fabric mounts itself to a rack with side release Fastex buckled compression straps. (Unfortunately, the straps and reflective triangle are designed in such a way that the bag is expected to be carried length-wise along the rack. Touring cyclists rarely carry gear this way. Tent, pad and bag are normally packed perpendicular to the rack.)

And then there are the panniers. They look at first like Kirtland packs; a pocket in the elasticized hood, held securely in place by a single vertical strap with side release Fastex buckle, two horizontal compression straps, and exterior pockets on both sizes of the rear panniers—four on the "Trail Ridge," eight (!) on the "Butte Mountain." Kangaroo uses a tough "weatherproof 11 ounce ballistic nylon," said to have been found by an independent testing lab to be "66% more abrasion resistant than Cordura." The top suspension hooks are coated (like Kirtland and Madden) to avoid marring the finish on anodized racks, and are attached to the bags by means of an aluminum stiffener.

Kangaroo has developed an original "Fail-Safe Mounting System," which employs a cross-strap configuration of nylon webbing. The biker engages two metal rings (located at the bottom rear of the pack) on the lower rack support ends, or slips the cross-straps around the flat bottom of low-rider racks, and lifts the bag onto its suspension hooks. He then reaches between the wheel and rack to find the finger loops at the end of either strap, and pulls them taut. Fastex three-bar slides hold the tension, while the nylon straps velcro in place to stay out of the spokes. (I had some difficulty at first in these adjustments, as my hands again found the space between racks and wheels to be rather tight.)

The bags are not designed to snap together when off the bike, D-rings exist for shoulder straps, and nylon handles are sewn into the top of every pack. The large "Tioga" handlebar bag also has D-rings for easy carrying, and a removable map case. Like Kirtland, there is no facility for making these bags into backpacks.

Madden:

A clean looking, easy to mount, extremely tough system. No compression straps on the front and rear panniers (and thus no fear of snagging brush), no exterior pockets, nor any strap-and-buckle hood to be released for entry into each pack's only compartment. Instead, a huge #10 YKK coil double slide zipper is at the top of each bag. Newest models have exterior pockets on the rear panniers, and—a *great* design modification—an extension of the zipper entry down the rear side of each bag. This last feature allows for greater access to contents. Extremely tough "WaterLok"-treated 11.5 ounce Cordura nylon is used, with one inch wide rain flaps over each zipper.

Like the appearance, the mounting system is also clean and easy. An "S" hook is engaged on the bottom rack support strut, and the bag is lifted onto its coated suspension hooks. (The hooks in turn are attached through the bag to an aluminum stiffener by means of screws and nyloc nuts.) Two nylon straps (on the rear packs, one wide strap on the front) which are sewn onto the top back of the bag are then used to engage a buckle next to each suspension hook; the strap is quickly slipped into the one-bar buckle (thereby enclosing the top support tube of the rack) and velcroed back into place. It is fast, and proved to be secure as well.

But now comes the greatest novelty of the Madden "Rough Rider Pannier System." Along the top perimeter of each rear pannier is a zipper; its purpose is to attach a huge rear "sleeping bag compartment" made of the same WaterLok-treated nylon Cordura. Two compression straps sit across this huge compartment, and can be used (as I have done) to help secure a tent. The top bag has a second zippered compartment on its underside; herein are hidden the two padded shoulder straps which turn this versatile bag into a rucksack. When on one's back the two compression straps lie horizontally, and thus can serve to hold extra clothing. (This zipper design has been replaced by snaps in later models.)

I have to hand it to this company for originality in design. (See Chapter Four for comments on their "Omni" system.) Frankly, I prefer the lack of straps and buckles on the face of each pannier, the ease of entry and simple mounting system. In fact, I've noticed only two drawbacks to the bags. The first is the relatively small capacity of the rear panniers. While this space is greatly enhanced by the huge top pack, that pack is designed to hold a sleeping bag, *not* the gear one might need to get to while touring. I tried separating those items I felt assured would not be needed until I'd stopped for the night and packing them into the top bag. Then I strapped my sleeping bag and tent on top, and rode like that for a few days.

But there's the problem. How many items is a touring cyclist certain he'll not require before camp? And if bulky spare clothing is stored in this top pannier, the tent and sleeping bag are raised even farther above the rack, thus reducing stability. My hope is that Madden will enlarge their rear panniers to the size of their competitors; the top pack then could be used solely for one's sleeping bag.

The second drawback I've noticed is the lack of a place for those items one wishes to keep separate from other gear like sunglasses, wallet, etc. Madden does not make a handlebar bag in its "Rough Rider" line, and the lack of even one exterior pocket on the panniers is troublesome to me at times. However, the company does put out two more items I should mention: a "Field Office"—a large wallet affair that holds passport, credit cards and cash, pen and small notepad, and which velcroes closed and also around one's belt; and a "Cyclist Emergency Kit" with sixteen survival items—tube tent, waterproof matches, dextrose and first aid supplies. But don't forego the other medical supplies I've discussed, as this kit and all the rest aren't built to handle *real* road wounds.

Needle Works:

I haven't yet tested this company's mountain line. But it appears the panniers are made with all the care in construction and choice of materials that goes into their touring bags. Eleven ounce Cordura is used, with internal stiffeners of 6061-T6 aluminum and polyethylene. Coated suspension hooks attach to these stiffeners with allen head bolts and nyloc nuts. Two straps with Fastex quick-release fasteners, finger loops, and velcro ends hold the bag securely to the stable Gordon racks; one mounts horizontally across the back of the pack, the second pulls diagonally. (These "Odyssey" panniers are designed for use with the amazingly stable Bruce Gordon racks only.) Interior seam binding, internal dividers (taking the place of external pockets), and triple compression straps are present, plus dual rain flaps, handles at the top of each bag and shoulder strap buckles for off-bike carrying.

The owner/designer of this company called recently to say he'd developed a solution to the problem of the costly repairs necessitated when branches or sharp rocks poke holes in the bottom of panniers. He has now developed a snug-fitting cover made of the same weight Cordura, enveloping all but the very backside of the bag. While this will surely handle the problems of riding rough trails, it does nothing for accessibility—that pervasive rear pannier trouble brought on by top-loading systems and wide loads on racks.

The above was written *before* my second long all-terrain tour of '84...a two thousand mile fall/winter run. Bob Beckman of Needle Works called while I was preparing for the ride to offer his new style of ATB panniers. The design had changed to that of his touring line—front loading, internally divided bags. Two extremely long double zippers (huge YKK stainless steel slides and pulls) run across the top of each bag; when fully unzipped the pannier falls open easily to allow excellent access to contents—even while one's rear rack is fully loaded. Construction, hardware and materials used are also similar to this company's fine touring line, but Needle Works has gone one step further to make its bags impervious. Waterproof Cordura rain covers are offered for the ultimate in protection. The cover's bottom third is a weave and fabric which is even tougher than the top, to turn away those obstacles which otherwise might puncture one's pannier. Thus, while in the roughest parts of trails, in the rain and snow and even while in town (such total coverings discourage casual theft) I rode with covers on.

The covers, like the bags, come in a color scheme of red and black. This makes them very visible to motorists (especially important while commuting), and helps them stand out nicely in slides shot during rides. A drawstring closure holds the cover in place, and a convenient velcro strap prevents the drawstring cord from getting caught in spokes.

When the bike bag companies read these words I'm sure I'll hear of the good points I've failed to mention, and design changes already on the boards. My defense will be that I'm not attempting to present my readers with a catalogue, but with a quick comparison which can serve only as a *beginning* in their search for the right panniers.

Mountain Bike Bags:

Kangaroo Baggs
3891 North Ventura Avenue
Ventura, CA 93001

Kirtland
Hine/Snowbridge, Inc.
P. O. Box 4059
Boulder, CO 80306

Lone Peak Designs Ltd.
3474 South 2300 East
Salt Lake City, Utah 84109

Madden USA
2400 Central Avenue
Dept. MB4
Boulder, CO 80301

Needle Works
769 Monroe Street
Eugene, OR 97402

(Addresses of other items mentioned in text)

The Coleman Company, Inc.
445 N. Minnesota
Wichita, KS 67214

Edwards Ski Products
2109 West 2300 South
Salt Lake City, Utah 84119

Moss Tent Works
Box 309 E
Camden, ME 04843

Spenco Medical Corporation
Box 8113
Waco, Texas 76710

CycleTote
640 West 3rd Street
Loveland, CO 80537

Specialized
844 Jury Court
San Jose, CA 95112

TREK Bicycle Corporation
810 W. Madison Street
P.O. Box 183
Waterloo, WI 53594

Shimano
9530 Cozycroft Avenue
Chatsworth, CA 91311

SunTour
10 Madison Road
Fairfield, NJ 07006

Precor USA
9449 151st Avenue N.E.
Redmond, WA 98052

Bruce Gordon Racks
1070 West 2nd Avenue
Eugene, OR 97402

Blackburn
75 Cristich Lane
Campbell, CA 95008

Cannondale Corp.
9 Brookside Place
Georgetown, CT 06829

Eclipse, Inc.
P.O. Box 7370
Ann Arbor, MI 48107

APPENDIX D

Topographic maps are of tremendous value to *any* biker, but are of even greater importance to the all-terrain trail rider or cycle tourist. Service station maps are made for motorists, and only topos will tell you if you'll be climbing mountains or simply rolling across plains. Such information is of critical importance; use it to help determine your food and water needs. Remember that you're on your own much more when you're off-road.

Begin by writing to one of the addresses below to request an index to the topographic maps of the area you'll be touring, a price list, and the booklet *Topographic Maps*. (The booklet explains how to read topos; it's *very* simple.) Next, order maps from the following offices:

(for "areas east of the Mississippi River, including Minnesota, Puerto Rico and the Virgin Islands of the United States,")

Branch of Distribution
U.S. Geological Survey
1200 South Eads Street
Arlington, VA 22202

(for "areas west of the Mississippi River, including Alaska, Hawaii, Louisiana, American Somoa, and Guam")

Branch of Distribution
U.S. Geological Survey
P.O. Box 25286
Federal Center
Denver, CO 80225

APPENDIX E

Below and following are "blow-up" diagrams of derailleur sets, a cantilever brake assembly, and a front chainwheel. They are included here for two reasons. First, though they are provided courtesy of Shimano, and are of their components, they can be useful when working on any manufacturer's equipment. Second, they serve as an example of the type of illustrations which should come with your equipment when you purchase it, or which can be obtained from bike shops or manufacturers. When using these diagrams be patient and note each part as it is removed so that reassembly is made easier. Manufacturers' names for specific parts will of course vary, so be open to that when comparing these diagrams to your bike.

SERVICE INSTRUCTION

Model FC-6206 Front Chainwheel

- Model BB-6207 Bottom Bracket Assembly
- Model CR-BP10 Biopace Chainring

● SHIMANO

■ **Assembly**

Assembly of Bottom Bracket Section

1) Apply a little grease to the right hand cup threads, and screw the cup anticlockwise into the bottom bracket. Then tighten up this cup using the tool (A) (TL-FC30). Apply a force by hand up to 35 — 40 kg (77-88 lbs.) by gripping the spanner 20 cm (7-7/8") from its end.

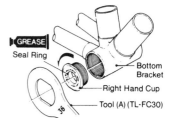

GREASE
Seal Ring
Bottom Bracket
Right Hand Cup
Tool (A) (TL-FC30)

Right hand cup tightening torque: 700-800 kgfcm (600-690 in. lbs.)

2) Apply enough grease to the ball retainers. Install them onto each side of the bottom bracket spindle, and put them into the bottom bracket from left side. Next, apply grease to the left hand cup threads and assemble this cup and the lock ring.

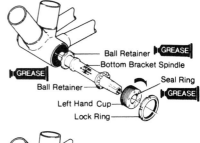

Ball Retainer GREASE
Bottom Bracket Spindle
GREASE
Seal Ring
Ball Retainer
GREASE
Left Hand Cup
Lock Ring

3) Using the tools (B) and (C) (TL-FC30), adjust the left hand cone to eliminate any play. Next tighten up the lock ring.

Note: The sealed mechanism makes it difficult to detect spindle play. Be sure to check carefully.

Lock ring tightening torque:

700-800 kgfcm (600-690 in. lbs.)

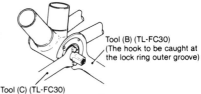

Tool (B) (TL-FC30) (The hook to be caught at the lock ring outer groove)

Tool (C) (TL-FC30) (The two pins to be engaged into the left hand cup holes)

Crank Assembly

1) Set the right hand crank to the right
   side of the bottom bracket spindle.
   Screw the crank fixing bolt onto the
   bottom bracket spindle by means of
   the cotterless crank tool (TL-F10)
   and a 17 mm spanner.
   Secure the left hand crank the same
   way.

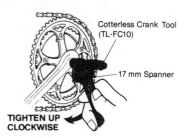

Cotterless Crank Tool
(TL-FC10)

17 mm Spanner

**TIGHTEN UP
CLOCKWISE**

Crank fixing bolt tightening torque: 250-350 kgfcm (220-300 in. lbs.)

2) Place and tighten up the right and left
   crank caps with the 5 mm hexagon
   wrench (TL-WR35).

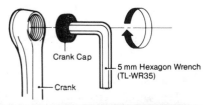

Crank Cap

5 mm Hexagon Wrench
(TL-WR35)

Crank

Biopace Chainring Assembly

● **Setting Chainrings**

Teeth number
indication

➡ **Out**

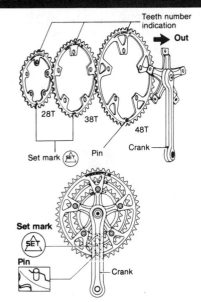

1) Set each chainring with teeth number
   indication facing out.

28T

38T

48T

Crank

Set mark (SET)   Pin

2) Install each chainring with set mark
   and pin aligned with the crank.

Set mark

(SET)

Pin

Crank

SERVICE INSTRUCTION

SHIMANO DEORE
XT Series

Cantilever Brake

BR-MC70 Cantilever Brake
BL-M700 Brake Lever

■ Exploded View and Parts List

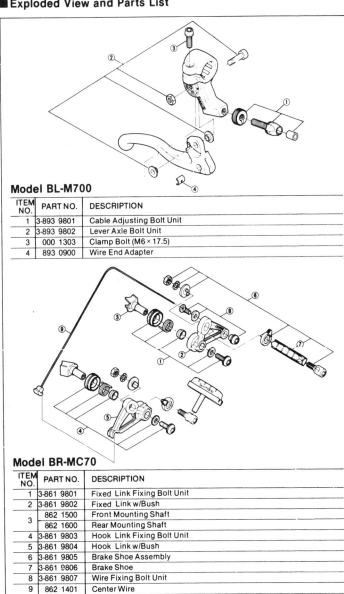

Model BL-M700

ITEM NO.	PART NO.	DESCRIPTION
1	3-893 9801	Cable Adjusting Bolt Unit
2	3-893 9802	Lever Axle Bolt Unit
3	000 1303	Clamp Bolt (M6 × 17.5)
4	893 0900	Wire End Adapter

Model BR-MC70

ITEM NO.	PART NO.	DESCRIPTION
1	3-861 9801	Fixed Link Fixing Bolt Unit
2	3-861 9802	Fixed Link w/Bush
3	862 1500	Front Mounting Shaft
3	862 1600	Rear Mounting Shaft
4	3-861 9803	Hook Link Fixing Bolt Unit
5	3-861 9804	Hook Link w/Bush
6	3-861 9805	Brake Shoe Assembly
7	3-861 9806	Brake Shoe
8	3-861 9807	Wire Fixing Bolt Unit
9	862 1401	Center Wire

SERVICE INSTRUCTION

SHIMANO DEORE
XT Series   **Derailleur set**

RD-M700	Rear Derailleur
FD-M700	Front Derailleur
SL-M700	Shifting Lever

□ Exploded View and Parts List

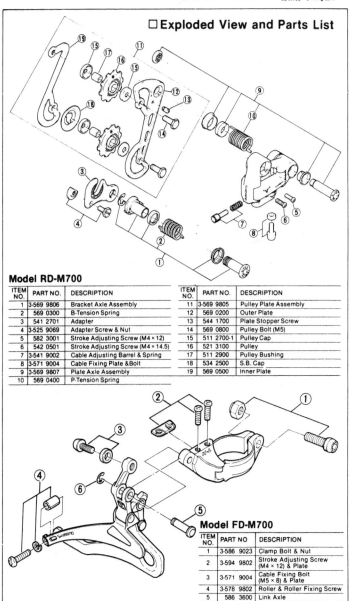

Model RD-M700

ITEM NO.	PART NO.	DESCRIPTION	ITEM NO.	PART NO.	DESCRIPTION
1	3-569 9806	Bracket Axle Assembly	11	3-569 9805	Pulley Plate Assembly
2	569 0300	B-Tension Spring	12	569 0200	Outer Plate
3	541 2701	Adapter	13	544 1700	Plate Stopper Screw
4	3-525 9069	Adapter Screw & Nut	14	569 0800	Pulley Bolt (M5)
5	582 3001	Stroke Adjusting Screw (M4 × 12)	15	511 2700-1	Pulley Cap
6	542 0501	Stroke Adjusting Screw (M4 × 14.5)	16	521 3100	Pulley
7	3-541 9002	Cable Adjusting Barrel & Spring	17	511 2900	Pulley Bushing
8	3-571 9004	Cable Fixing Plate & Bolt	18	534 2500	S.B. Cap
9	3-569 9807	Plate Axle Assembly	19	569 0500	Inner Plate
10	569 0400	P-Tension Spring			

Model FD-M700

ITEM NO.	PART NO	DESCRIPTION
1	3-586 9023	Clamp Bolt & Nut
2	3-594 9802	Stroke Adjusting Screw (M4 × 12) & Plate
3	3-571 9004	Cable Fixing Bolt (M5 × 8) & Plate
4	3-578 9802	Roller & Roller Fixing Screw
5	586 3600	Link Axle
6	582 3600	Stop Ring

Dennis Coello has spent his adult life on a bicycle. Raised in St. Louis, he has pedalled around the world and has lived without an automobile for fifteen years. He is the author of three previous books on the subject including *Bicycle Touring in Utah* and the forthcoming *Bicycle Touring in Arizona*, two in a series of state guides Dream Garden Press will be publishing over the next several years.